CW00566623

WORDS MADE FLESH

Ramsey Dukes

70/550

WORDS MADE FLESH

or

INFORMATION IN FORMATION

Artificial intelligence, humanity, and the cosmos

Ramsey Dukes

THE MOUSE THAT SPINS
WINCHESTER

British Library Cataloguing in Publication Data

Dukes Ramsey
Words made flesh: artificial intelligence,
man and cosmos.
1. Technology - Philosophical perspectives
I. Title
601

ISBN 0 904311 06 6

First published in 1988 by The Mouse That Spins,
Wharf Mill, Winchester, Hants SO23 9NJ

Copyright © TMTS, 1988

Designed and produced by Creative Technology Associates,
'Yan Shang Po', Water Lane, Somerton, Somerset TA11 6RG

Set in 9 on 10 point Times with Apple™ Macintosh
equipment and Aldus PageMaker™ 3.0

Made and printed by Castle Cary Press, Castle Cary, Somerset

Conditions of Sale
This book is sold subject to the condition
that it shall not, by way of trade or otherwise,
be lent, re-sold, hired out or otherwise circulated
without the publisher's prior consent in any form of
binding or cover other than that in which it is
published and without a similar condition
including this condition being imposed
on the subsequent purchaser.

Contents

Preface

READERS WHO KNOW my other writings will find this book a little different in style: it was originally intended for a wider public, and I hoped to earn some money from royalties as a result. But the process of finding a publisher is painfully slow, and I want to get these ideas off my hands before they grow stale and hold up other projects.

One of the snags of presenting this particular text to a typical occult publisher is that it seems to be waging an old war: it presents a challenge to the traditional materialist world view. However, many occultists think this is no longer necessary, arguing that science itself has now defeated that materialist model of reality. I agree there has been a revolution, but think that the revolution has been at a comparatively 'high' level and that it has not yet filtered down through society and through our psyches.

This is how I see that 'high' revolution. When Uranus entered Capricorn early this century, certain appropriately revolutionary (ie Uranian) ideas about the physical world (ie Capricorn) were suggested by Einstein and others. They were probably viewed with suspicion by the scientific establishment. But a quarter of the way through the century those ideas were being taken quite seriously by the scientists and were beginning to get some exposure to a wider public who perhaps began hearing about "this loony scientist who thinks that you grow old faster if you move very quickly".

By half way through the century there had been dramatic evidence for the new theories: they were pretty well established as the new scientific world-view. The man in the street now knew they 'must' be true, but could not really believe it. By the late sixties everyone knew that relativity and quantum physics was 'true' and that matter, space and time were nothing like as solid as we used to believe. This is what was being taught in the classrooms, this is what was being said in the media, and so this is what we knew in our intellects to be 'true'. However, our bodies and our souls still did not believe it. We still acted as if this world was solid and real, our emotional attachments to the world were still largely unshaken.

In 1988 Uranus once more entered Capricorn to shake our view of material reality: the cycle has gone full circle. There is now a significant number of scientists and 'new age' thinkers who seem to have fully assimilated the new models of existence with all their mystery and uncertainty – the idea has filtered down from pure intellect to take a hold on their whole being. But there are many more who claim to accept these ideas, but who do not live as if they fully accepted them in body and soul as well as intellect. A new generation is finding it easier to live with the new reality, but to the majority of people over 30 these scientific ideas as somehow very 'remote from reality'. Our bodies and souls still live in a materialist world.

That is what I mean by a 'high level' revolution. It began with an intellectual elite, and it depends for its verification on subtle processes in highly exclusive and expensive laboratories. At the personal level we hear about these developments with our ears, and so we learn to accept them in a very 'left brain' intellectual fashion. The rest of our being remains sceptical.

But in this book I predict a new revolution at the gut level. I propose that contact with a coming generation of computers will trigger that revolution; that in a few years' time you will be able to go into an electronics game arcade and come out with severe doubts about the nature of this reality we inhabit. This will not be an elite intellectual revolution, it will be a gut-level one. It will not be spread by books and lectures on science or computing, but by computer games and science fiction fantasy films. It will speak directly to our souls.

I suspect this revolution will spread more rapidly for having by-passed our intellects. It will be upon us before we 'know' what has happened. This book tries to prepare us for the change.

My own interest in this revolution is twofold: that it will profoundly alter our ideas about magic, and that it will revolutionise the individual's place in society. It will do so by making this universe into a connected whole, instead a concretion of separate parts.

Most 'new age' philosophies argue that this world is a connected whole, but none have really managed to find a satisfactory model for that connectedness. 'Morphic fields' have been proposed, but the word 'field' has a definite scientific significance which does not seem appropriate to the theory suggested - morphic fields do not seem to relate to space in a field-like manner. What is wanted is a model of the universe in which information is more fundamental than space, time or matter.

The revolution I predict will drop us right into such a model of the universe.

Of course, I could be wrong - and that would elevate this work from mere speculation into real science fiction!

The Minister For Technology and The Pope - 1

THERE WAS BRILLIANT SUNLIGHT in the Council Room, and there was utter silence.

As John Stephens, Minister for Technology, entered he made note of who else was present, and who was absent, before bowing curtly to the throne and taking his seat. As usual, the War Minister and the Chancellor were already seated close to the King. Although expected, this was nevertheless a snub, implying a previous, higher meeting to which the Minister of Technology was now summoned. But at least the Pope was absent: that would make things easier for John, who appreciated the present King's increasing tendency to overlook the fourth of his Prime Ministers.

"JS has something important to announce". The King raised his head and fixed his gaze on the distant statue of Justice beyond the Palace roofs. On coronation he had had the Council room rearranged to make this possible, declaring that the symbol of Justice with her scales was profoundly inspiring to decisions of state, whilst admitting to himself that his resulting posture, with head raised and distant gaze, would look impressively regal.

It also meant, on this occasion, that He did not have to look his Minister for Technology in the eye. Despite a public popularity second only to the Pope's, John Stephens was at close quarters subtly but unpleasantly abrasive. A fighter, and a curious contrast to the War Minister: Irma was feared and respected as a formidable soldier and yet there was a comforting sense of firmness and reliability about her presence in the Council Room. Least popular of all was his "leaden wet blanket" of a Chancellor; and yet Mavis was like a mother to him. In the ghastly freeze of last winter He would never have dared suggest diverting money from the railway programme to improve the palace heating; but Mavis had pushed it through. Funnily enough, the Pope was quite nice too. Pity really. Yes, pity about the Pope. And John was still going on about the completion of M Project when Irma interrupted.

"But you've said nothing more about its suitability for military use - the whole purpose of the project."

"Or at least the justification for the unprecedented investment" added the Chancellor, stealing John's obvious rejoinder.

"It has always been made perfectly clear that the Macrocomputer would so outstrip the performance of any existing system, that it would give us an immense tactical advantage in terms of predicting enemy movements. But it can only be as good as the intelligence already gathered for it" spoken sharply." And the effort required to re-program so much information about the universe could take at least six months."

The Chancellor tutted, the War Minister frowned, and the Minister for Technology added "unless there was special motivation, some extra incentive for the programmers. Which brings me to the main point of my presentation".

'Wait for it', thought the King, 'the inevitable sting in the tail: it's all complete but just needing another few million and another few months to make it actually work'.

The Minister for Technology rose to his feet, for added impact, and cleared his throat. "Macroc can provide the ultimate solution to the religious problem. And it will only take three weeks."

He had surprised them, even the King was looking at him now. Before anyone could interrupt John continued.

"How often have you, Irma, regretted at this table that you are fighting an enemy apparently unhampered by the religious superstitions which infect so many of our soldiers? How often have you, Mavis, regretted the public money and wasted man-hours spent on religious festivals? How often have I complained of low morale in my own ministry in face of the tide of public superstition?

"And..." saving the biggest carrot for last... "anyone who studies the public mood will have noted that the more the Pope is excluded from Council, the more the public is inclined to see their supposed 'God' as an alternative authority to the King."

"But allow me just three weeks longer with Macroc, and all that will be ended."

"Not that silly robot priest again?" twittered Mavis.

"NO!" John flushed with irritation. "Why does it always come back to that? If I have to say it a hundred times, I'll say it once more: my only involvement with the robot priest was to write a paper predicting that the project would fail, simply because it totally misunderstood the basic philosophical foundations of religious belief. The very reason why this present proposition is bound to succeed."

Sitting down once more, he began to outline his plan. He was very persuasive, possibly because he had polished his speech by meticulously rehearsing it into a Personalised Response Profile of his audience, run on Macroc.

1
Introduction

In the 1960s a book was published called *Chariots of the Gods* by Erik von Däniken. The book got its title from the author's suggestion that this planet might in the past have been visited by spacecraft from a more advanced culture, and that this possibility could not only explain a large number of universal myths, but also explain a number of puzzling archealogical discoveries.

The book caused quite a stir. It also invoked a cynical reaction in the popular scientific press, which soon began to see von Däniken as a more or less blinkered crank who would do anything to fit the facts to his own rigid beliefs. Apparently, respected authorities had analysed von Däniken's factual evidence and found it inadequate, unconfirmed, or even false.

But when I later read the original book, I was agreeably surprised. For the main message of the book seemed not to be dogmatic, but rather to be an appeal for a less blinkered approach, a call for greater imagination when trying to explain the findings of archeaology. The 'Chariots of the Gods' idea was proposed not as a final solution, but as a hypothesis that ought to be tested, rather than dismissed without consideration.

The fact that this challenge prompted such antagonism was curious. Especially as the commonest reaction was not to respond to the basic challenge - the attack on academic dogmatism - but rather to turn it back on the challenger and accuse von Däniken himself of being dogmatic.

Is von Däniken a dogmatic crank? How would I know? I have never met him. Perhaps I should read his later books to find out? But if I found them dogmatic and cranky, unlike his first book, then I would not know whether this was a revelation of his true nature, or simply his bitter reaction to early criticism. In effect I would not know whether the critical reaction to his ideas had unmasked him, or corrupted him.

The answer to this dilemma concerns me as a human, but I must now pass it by. For this book is not about such answers, it is more concerned with the pattern of action and reaction that took place between von Däniken and his detractors - a pattern which suggests deep currents of feeling being disguised as academic debate.

I have elsewhere proposed the study of what I called 'metascience'[1]. The idea of metascience is to study the behaviour and utterances of those who have attained a high level of expertise in any subject. If that study reveals certain predictable patterns amongst experts, then the study is highly worthwhile; because this knowledge could prove more economical than either consulting the experts, or becoming experts ourselves. The one science of 'knowing what sort of answers are always given by experts when consulted', could replace all the existing sciences, provided it could achieve a good enough level of prediction.

Actually, this proposal is not as revolutionary as it sounds, because it is not as simple as it seems. Many people find it easier to persue an academic study for ten years, than once grasp the possibility that inspired ignorance could prove as effective as knowledge in the struggle to survive.

The importance that I see in von Däniken's work lies not in whether he is right or wrong, whether he is wise or crazy, but rather in the fact that his books belong to a fine tradition of public 'mind-bogglers'. Von Däniken, Velikovsky, the Bermuda Triangle, Adamski, Uri Geller... names to conjure with when the conversation amongst friends turns from the everyday towards the unknown. Each a falling star that has briefly shone in the friction of its contact with the upper intellectual atmosphere. 'But how many have fallen to earth?' asks the cynic.

I propose that the shining is more important than the falling; that the light is worth more than the material evidence.

In fact I am trying to write just another such book.

Why?

I remember as a child my excitement on reading George Adamski's first book on flying saucers[2]; I remember enjoying the public excitement as his ideas were discussed in the press and on television. I also recall a certain bitterness when the establishment refused to be rocked; when Adamski's evidence *was* rocked; and when later books of that current went 'over the top' and asked me to swallow more wonders than my worldview would allow. I wanted an allopathic dose of mystery, but not a killer dose.

In effect I felt a little cheated. Cheated, but eager to recoup my money's worth, as it were.

Anyone who has fallen for a cheat (let us say he is walking away twenty pounds light from the three-card players that haunt the back streets around London's Piccadilly Circus) can either wallow in anger and self-pity, or else recoup his loss by reviewing his experience in a broader context. The three card player could see his loss as an interesting brush with London's Underworld, as a Lesson in Life, as a good story to tell his mates, and so on. In other words, an experience well worth the money it cost.

In my case, I did not regret Adamski, because my contact with his ideas had been stimulating. It had opened my soul to the thrill of being a battlefield for two Cosmic Forces.

One Force wanted me to retain my grasp on the known facts. The other Force wanted me to leap out and embrace greater mysteries.

One Force pointed backward to Established Reality. The other pointed forward to a New Myth.

In the terminology of my earlier work[3], I was standing in a 'Scientific' worldview, and one Force (named 'commonsense') was drawing me back to a 'Religious' worldview where God's word (in the form of scientific authority and the absolute of objective reality) could not be challenged. The other Force (a spirit of adventure, let's call it 'the Aquarian Impulse') said that I was outgrowing the accepted scientific myth and needed to reach forward to a larger myth to live by.

That is how I see it. But others would reverse the direction and argue that the first 'Force' was the *forward* pull toward a rational, verifiable worldview, while the second 'Force' was a *backward* pull to a more primitive, emotional or mythic worldview. Elsewhere[4] I have defended my view of the direction of evolution: what really matters here is that the overall, long term effect of my contact with Adamski's ideas seemed more positive than negative.

What I would like to propose is that such ideas, and therefore such books as I have mentioned, are in fact more of a positive stimulus than a bad influence.

This would make me feel better about writing another such book.

Although we mostly have an idea of a 'real world', as we call it, most of the time we live on mental maps of that world rather than whole-heartedly within it: total sensory awareness is not the normal everyday state, instead it is something that has to be deliberately practiced in certain schools of meditation. If I am walking through London, then I am usually in a slightly withdrawn state, seeing my progress on a mental map of my surroundings. If I am on a shopping trip my mental map of London will be different from the map of London in my mind when I am sitting in the country and trying to decide if I would like to live in London. Walking down familiar or predictable streets we are more aware of our inner map than the actual street - until something surprising happens. Only if, for example, something happens to make me believe I am lost or dreaming, do I snap out of my current map and take a hard look at the street I am in, as if seeing it for the first time: the street has been pedestrianised and I am momentarily lost, my senses are suddenly fully alert until I 'find my bearings', that is to say I must revise my familiar map before I can relax into it once more.

There is an enormous choice of maps, and the maps take many forms. Any scheme that not only divides reality into categories or areas, but also assumes and presents a pattern of relationship between those areas, is a map. The Times Atlas is a map of our world, but so also is the Zodiac. A site plan of a factory is a map of it, but so also is a 'tree diagram' illustrating the company's departmental structure. A road map is a map of England, but so also is the idea that England consists of just three areas: Greater London, provincial cities, and rural England.

Many arguments between people arise from a mistaken feeling that you can always superimpose maps directly. Try to place the underground map of London over the street map, and it simply does not fit. Ask which signs of the Zodiac are supposed to represent rural England, and you cannot expect a clear-cut answer.

What I want to suggest is that the excitement of the 'mind boggler' is that it gives you an interesting new map of the world. And it is always stimulating to explore with a new map.

Attend a talk on the latest popular psychological theory, attend a meeting of a new religious cult, read a book that suggests exciting new possibilities about the world's history, and you come away either cynical or else with an intriguing new map. 'After reading that book on Transactional Analysis I can see so much more in our relationship' you hear people say. As time passes this map could prove so useful that its features will be copied onto many of your other maps. But all too often the new map gradually falls into disuse because it is irrelevent or because it does not seem to fit the 'real world'. (Elsewhere[5] I have discussed the idea that the 'real world' is itself just another map).

For most people the 'mind boggler' books I have mentioned are in the last category: they presented ideas that were stimulating for a while, but were later apparently disproved and forgotten. For this reason their bitterest critics would say that such books are a bad influence, affording cheap stimulation by appealing to the public love of sensation. I would counter that by drawing an analogy with the pills and potions prescribed by doctors: although there are good arguments against their abuse, it is folly to ignore the relief that they have afforded to millions.

If I am to write a new 'mind boggler', I am aware that there are some people for whom it will bring a little excitement, mystery and challenge into their lives. Even if this is only a fleeting effect, it could still prove worthwhile. If it lasts longer, it might utterly transform their lives. Later in this book I will explain how.

How can I help the stimulating effect to last? One way is to base the argument not on facts, but on a direction of movement. Any book based upon facts is at the mercy of those investigators who excel at the art of invoking uncertainties - ironically enough, these people are usually themselves the High Priests of Absolute Certainty. When academics preface every bit of evidence with such cautious phrases as 'investigations seem to confirm that...', they are defending their reputations, not their theses. Any evidence is liable to be falsified by a sufficiently determined investigator.

A book that says not 'this is so', but rather 'if A happens then B will be so' can only be condemned by Time or Logic.

The book you are reading will begin by noting a disturbing trend in our thinking. True, it will then argue for the existence of that trend, and for the likelihood of its continuation, but this is not the real point of the book: this is only done in order to make things sound more relevant, and so more exciting.

Next the book looks at the likely outcome of that trend, and argues that the likely outcome is much more interesting than many people fear. So this is a piece of prediction, not a statement of arguable fact. So, if it cannot be attacked on grounds of 'bad evidence', how can it go wrong? Perhaps this second section could be attacked on logical grounds? That would be possible only if it presented a logical case. If the case is not logical, then logical argument can only state as much; it cannot say whether that part of the book is good or bad.

How are we to judge a work of prediction that is not based upon logical argument? We either wait and see, or else we judge it in a way that will be described in a later chapter of this book itself.

So here we have a book that opens with a attempt to justify its own existence, and closes with a description of how the reader ought to judge the book's own worth.

Such narcissism may not be in good taste, but it is a subtle illustration of the book's main argument.

Read on!

The Minister For Technology and The Pope - 2

Does he always keep his caravan so bloody cold?' the Minister for Technology wondered, plunging hands deep into the warmth of his trouser pockets. "Look, this is a straight challenge, at least that is how the public will see it" he slyly added. "If you're afraid your faith can't stand the test, that's your problem."

The Pope was using old newspaper to clean a frying pan; glancing over its rim he beamed. "I've got it! A new improved robot priest!"

"Oh for God's sake..." John exploded in exasperation.

"For who's sake?" the Pope innocently enquired.

Leaning back against the panelling and speaking wearily to the skylight, John ignored the question. "'To summarise: the Robot Priest Project is not only based upon a total lack of appreciation of the philosophical and psychological foundations of religious belief, it is also an insult to millenia of human tradition that is still to this day honoured by representation among the four Prime Ministers of this realm'. Those were my own words, or something very close, of twenty years ago. Quite apart from retaining my desire not to insult you, I also have no intention of making a fool of myself, like my predecessors did. The challenge remains. So, would you care to hear the details?"

The frying pan clanged foolishly against a bulkhead as the Pope shrugged his arms. The Minister for Technology leaned forward and began to speak in earnest. He was, thanks to rehearsals into a Personalised Response Profile of the Pope, run on Macroc, most persuasive.

When he had finished, the Pope remained promisingly silent for several breaths, then spoke quietly.

"I only grudge you the time away from my flock. If it looks like being a waste, then I might back out. Or perhaps I shouldn't? In any case, I'll not give an answer until I've prayed for guidance."

'Dammit!' John cursed inwardly. 'Bloody God's decision!' Whatever it was that the Pope did on those occasions - tossing coins, counting yarrow stalks or whatever - it added up to the fact that his response was always less predictable than that of any other Minister. John had a sudden insight into why the Pope's continued position as a Prime Minister seemed such a threat. So he answered with the utmost charm.

"Why, of course. The last thing I want is for you to commit yourself before giving this matter the most careful consideration".

The tour of the Macroc site was complete. John Stephens dismissed the others and sat down at a table in the Interface Chamber with the Pope, and two cups of coffee.

"So, that is Macroc."

"Amazing" said the Pope. "An incredible achievement. And yet you're prepared to hand it all over to the warlords in a few weeks time?"

"The defence of the realm must always take precedence". John tried to speak with conviction, and the Pope took some comfort from his failure to do so.

"Anyway. I now want to make sure that we both clearly understand the nature of my challenge. So I will summarise the situation, and this time it goes on record for both of us." He switched on the recorder.

"Our basic argument against religion is as follows. Science has postulated, and has increasingly found evidence to confirm, that our universe and everything within it has been generated by chance interactions of elementary particles subject to the laws of physics (which laws can themselves be modelled as further 'elementary particles'), and that no 'God', 'Spirit' or other outside agency has had any part in this process."

The Pope interrupted. "Whereas I recognise a God who created those particles and laws in the first place."

"Certainly. And we in turn would argue that the question 'who put them there?' is meaningless, except as a symptom of man's instinct to project the form and content of his own mind onto the screen of inert matter.

"We further argue that mankind is evolving, and that recognition of the true material foundation of existence is the most sophisticated achievement of our evolving consciousness. So much so that less developed intellects are unable as yet to grasp its reality, and have instead continued to cling to man's primitive conception of a creative God.

"Surprisingly, this same delusion still thrives in a few comparatively sophisticated minds." John beamed at the Pope. "Why they should avoid facing the evidence is far from clear."

"Because it's been far from conclusive," growled the Pope.

"However, our final standpoint is as follows: no-one who has finally 'seen the light' and fully grasped the materialist explanation could possibly continue to believe in a needless deity. Even the more recent argument put forward by the 'neo-theological' movement, namely that God was real enough, but was himself a consequence of the interaction of elementary particles, has fallen by the wayside, because it placed God on the same level as ourselves, and challenged us to solve our problems without him.

"As you rightly say, there has until now been a lack of utterly conclusive evidence; and a number of overzealous scientists have made premature promises to provide such evidence, calling down public ridicule on the educated, materialist position."

"Like a robot priest which molested children?"

"Well, yes. But even there you could argue that he merely betrayed human weakness... But let's forget the damned robot priest!"

John Stephens checked the recorder and continued.

"Now, in Macroc, we have at last got the chance of proving our assertion. Because we have, for the first time, a computer large enough to model an entire universe, allowing us to witness the actual creation of that universe from its

elementary particles.

"Macroc has been programmed to recognise a four dimensional continuum, and the fundamental laws of physics which hold within it. Into this continuum it has generated a random distribution of particles corresponding in quality, and approximate quantity, to the initial cloud of hydrogen atoms preceding the Big Bang that created our own universe.

"Now Macroc is on 'hold'. When the command is given to run the program, I predict that a universe very much like our own will be modelled within Macroc. Millions of years of evolution will be reproduced in just two weeks of our time."

"I didn't understand one point. Why did you create a random cloud of particles, rather than trying to extrapolate back to the precise conditions of our own universe? Wouldn't that make a much more conclusive case, by recreating our own universe exactly as it is now?"

"I explained that we could never determine the precise condition of our own universe, on account of the Uncertainty Principle: a little device kindly inserted by God to make sure we don't ourselves get caught in any self-reflexive paradoxes!"

"Your God does certain things even better than my one" the Pope replied, and the Minister for Technology laughed.

"I'll make a convert of you yet! Anyway, one other preparation is needed. We must both put on scanner helmets and spend about three hours in a coma while Macroc reads the structure of our brains. Every element of our personalities will be encoded digitally to produce two 'human' programs to be stored in Macroc's memory. When they run we will live as conscious entities more or less 'within' the model universe being created inside Macroc, able to observe, and even to interact with it as one does in a dream. Also, just as when we dream, our physical bodies will remain in a coma, waiting until the memories of the 'dream' world are fed back into it."

"Hang on! I can't afford to waste three hours each day.."

"No. It's only an initial three hour scan. Your basic psyche will be held in memory. Next day you will indeed be different, but only different by an extra twenty-four hours of life experience. So the re-scan will only be a Difference Test, a bare five minutes on each subsequent occasion. And of course, at the end of each session, Macroc will hold you unconscious for a further five or so minutes in order to feed back to your real, physical brain; updating it so that you will remember everything that you experienced in the other Universe, just like waking from a vivid dream."

"Just how real is this dream going to feel?"

"Well you know what it's like in those arcade games..."

"I don't wast time on such things" snapped the Pope.

"Oh? You really ought to keep in touch with the way your flock are amusing themselves nowadays. Anyway, you almost certainly went into them as a kid, and you'll remember the old interactive 'Space Invaders' where you played out a battle which was pictured on a screen or as a 3-D holographic image with stereo sound effects. What they do now is more sophisticated: instead of playing the visual information on a screen it is transmitted direct to both optic nerves,

likewise the audio output goes direct to the inner ear, so you seem to be standing right in the battle, watching it with your own eyes and hearing it all around you. Now they even transmit the smells of battle and the tastes of banquets direct to the brain.

"But most important of all is the two-way transmission of signals between the game and the player's neural system. This means that the intention to, say, walk forward or to reach for a weapon in the battle will be picked up as motor impulses in the spinal nerve of the paralysed player, and the machine then calculates the appropriate sensation of walking through the battlefield and transmits it back to the same nerve. So you feel totally in the scene, just like a very vivid dream, while your real body lies in a semi coma in the games arcade booth. Marvelous gadgets those, a lot of my boys' research behind them.

"Anyway, to answer your question, that's the sort of reality to expect: it'll be like a very vivid dream of the sort where you know you are probably in a dream. In fact, you may need precautions to stop yourself getting quite lost in the dream, because Macroc is working at far higher definition than the crude arcade games - they're limited by commercial factors, plus legislation to stop kids getting totally out of touch, you know.

"Actually, that's another point: sensory governors. The system falls short of total reality because it doesn't allow sensory overload. If we are standing on a planet with a sulphur dioxide atmosphere, this program would allow us to suffer the burning smell, but not the resulting choking to death!"

"How comforting".

Seeing the Pope's puzzled frown John concluded. "Look, these technical details will grow clearer as we proceed. All I want to go on record is that I predict that what you are about to experience will be sufficient to shatter your faith. I would not predict that for the bulk of religious believers, because I don't think most of them are capable of grasping the full reality of what is about to happen. But you, the Pope, have a keen and sophisticated mind.

"I further surmise that any reluctance you have shown to go through with this experiment, is a symptom of the fact that you are intelligent enough to know I'm right."

The Pope chuckled. "If I thought it could hurt you, you'd be excommunicated this very instant."

The Minister for Technology indicated the recorder. "That too has gone on record!"

2
The Threat of Artificial Intelligence

IT WAS 1962, or thereabouts, and I was in the sixth form. In schools there is often some sort of organised extra-curricular discussion group to encourage the intellectuals - those not eligible to attend usually considered it a hotbed of 'pseuds', and sometimes they were right. Some of us sixth-formers used to attend a group which met occasionally to hear a talk or paper - often by a visiting speaker - and to spend the rest of the evening discussing it.

One week in the dining hall I overheard a teacher saying that the next visiting speaker was an interesting one: a man who believed that it might be possible to create a machine which could think like a human being. Apparently this man posed the question 'wWhy shouldn't a machine be able to have a sense of self-consciousness, or self-awareness?'

That question intrigued me. It seemed so obvious: of course a machine could never think like that. Why? Because it is only a machine!

It was the early days of computers, and we all knew that a cleverly-designed machine was perfectly capable of performing arithmetical calculations and other such 'mechanical' tasks, and capable of performing them faster than any human could. But we all knew that this ability bore no relation to real intelligence, let alone creativity.

In any case, by definition a machine could never think like a human. In the last paragraph I used the word 'mechanical' in just this sense: we describe something as 'mechanical' when it is performed without awareness. We use the word 'machine' to describe some thing that performs a task in just such a blind, unreasoning and unaware fashion. For example the phrase 'the publicity machine' is a double-edged one: on the one hand it is a compliment, implying something efficient, effective and dependable; on the other hand an insult that implies stupidity and predictability.

For reasons such as these it was at first obvious that the man must be talking nonsense. But somehow it wasn't quite as simple as that.

Consider the immediate tautological response: 'Of course a machine cannot think like a human - it is only a machine'. That depends upon the assumption that a human is not itself 'only a machine'. But humans spend a lot of their time performing 'mechanical' tasks; the 'publicity machine' is made up of human elements, so it must at least be possible for humans to think like machines. To carry this a step further: some philosophers, like Gurdjieff, argue that most of our thoughts and actions are largely mechanical, and that we only realise our true creative potential in rare moments, or as a result of intensive spiritual training. On that evidence we could predict that, although a machine is only a machine, it should be possible to make one which could imitate most of the thoughts and actions of the average human being. This would not totally vindicate the man's claim, but it would perhaps show that he was more right than wrong: we would almost have achieved what he claimed possible.

Now let us break out of the tautological trap that limits a machine's abilities by definition, and let us consider another question: is it possible that humans could, by using all the skills and abilities they possess, be able to create some object that thinks like themselves? In other words, we are now talking more generally about 'artificial intelligence' rather than 'machine intelligence'.

The answer now is obviously 'yes'. Because every time a couple produce a baby and educate it into an adult human, they have created something that thinks and acts like a human being, simply because it is a human being.

But perhaps that is not artificial enough? So what about the possibility of a test-tube baby? Would that count as artificial intelligence?

What about the possibility of going a stage further and somehow creating a culture of human brain cells *in vitro*? Would that count as artificial intelligence?

For reasons such as these I could see that my initial rejection of the idea was over-hasty. Instead of a clear distinction - a wide gulf between the minds of humans and the working of human artefacts - there was a considerable amount of overlap. On the one hand there was the fact that so much human thought was already mechanical; on the other hand there was the problem that, once you started to define a machine in more general terms than in terms of its own limitations, then suddenly you found yourself faced with all sorts of possibilities for the future.

That brief conversation overheard in the dining hall haunted me for days, so I decided to attend the next meeting and hear what this speaker had to say.

It was a good talk. The speaker, I think it was a 'Professor George' of Bristol University or somewhere, was introduced. He asked how long he was supposed to talk for, then proceeded to speak without notes for the exact time stated, presenting a strong and well-structured argument for his case. He did this so competently that later, amongst ourselves, we jokingly compared him to some sort of 'lecturing machine' designed to present an argument in any set timescale. But we all agreed that the machine had been designed to present the argument with wit and clarity!

I would like to stress this joke for several reasons. Once to point out that it was more a tribute to the excellence and precision of the talk ('mechanical' in the complimentary sense) than any suggestion that it was uninspired ('mechanical' in the derogatory sense). Secondly to point out that, by being so mechanically competent, the speaker was living out the truth of his own ideas - this is an important theme in the later stages of this book, and will be returned to. Thirdly to point out that we felt threatened by his talk, and that is why we needed to joke about it - a very English reaction!

If I attempted to recount what he said on that occasion, I might not do the speaker justice: both because it is not easy to remember words spoken over twenty years ago, but also because I may not be so good at expressing myself as he was. Instead of summarising the talk here, I will in the next chapter simply tackle some of the more obvious objections to artificial intelligence. What I want to consider now is the threat that his talk presented.

As explained earlier, my initial instinctive objection to machine intelligence was open to attack from two fronts. On the one hand there is the possibility that we may progress towards making artefacts so remarkable that they utterly transcend our present ideas of what constitutes a 'machine', and of what a machine's limitations must be. On the other hand there is also the possibility that we ourselves are already machines, albeit very complex ones.

The first possibility is an exciting one in that it opens up, or enlarges, our present world by suggesting that we may one day be able to do things now considered impossible: in other words we may be able to do what is now considered to be 'magic' (even if we will no longer see it as magic once we have achieved the ability). Whereas that first possibility enlarges our world the other possibility shrinks it, because it suggests that the transcendent 'specialness' which we believe sets us apart from machines, is only an illusion - it suggests that we are 'no more than' better machines. A whole dimension - the dimension that lies outside the possibilities of the machine universe - has been lopped from our perceived world.

It was this latter aspect of the argument that made his ideas so threatening; and this latter aspect was the core of his argument. It could hardly have been otherwise in a rational, intellectual context - where it is always far easier to shrink the world than to expand it.

If, for example, one is to present a truly rational argument to suggest that we will be able to do 'magic' in the future, then you have to be able to explain exactly how it will be done. In other words, you are forced to describe the greater world of the future in the limited language of our present, smaller, world. This cannot be done precisely. If, for example, I try to argue that we may one day be able to travel faster than light, I can present a vague argument based on the fact that mankind has repeatedly transcended limitations that were previously thought to be absolute; but this argument does not have a lot of strength against the person who expounds Einstein's theory of the absoluteness of the speed of light, then asks me to point out the flaw in the argument which will allow it to be transcended in the future.

If, on the other hand, you set about proving that the world is smaller than people believe, you need only define your own smaller world, then challenge others to prove that it is not the whole world. In other words you force others to try to describe the concepts that they believe to lie outside your smaller world, but to describe them in the limited vocabulary of the world you have defined. Now *they* have the impossible task!

On this occasion the latter approach was adopted by the speaker, quite unashamedly. 'What is there that a human can do that a machine could not do?' was his question. Then the typical answers were tackled one by one.

A machine could never write a poem?

But when is a poem not a poem? If I teach a computer the rules of English grammar, the idiomatic exceptions are fed into the memory, then the concepts of rhyme and meter are taught, why should it not produce a decent poem? Please define what is missing!

A machine can never create something new, surely it can only feed back what is put into it?

What do you mean by new? If I play chess against a computer, it is highly unlikely that the people who programmed it had anticipated the exact game that the machine and myself are now playing; instead they taught it the rules and some problem-solving techniques, and it is now creating new permutations of that information. What could be newer than that?

In each case the question is thrown back at the questioner with a demand to be more explicit. This is most obvious in the next example.

Surely a computer could never fall in love?

But I can program it to say 'I love you'!

But it wouldn't *really* be in love would it?

How do you know?

Someone really in love becomes all emotional...

But I can program a computer to start to make random errors, to malfunction when it senses your presence, to refuse to work unless you say you love it too...

As the speaker explained to our group, the argument is as follows:

- He claims that there is nothing a human can do or experience that a machine will not eventually be able to duplicate, and challenges us to prove otherwise.

- Whenever we propose an example, like falling in love, he replies by asking us for a precise description of that example.

- But his conception of a precise description is that it must be a totally logical and therefore a mechanical description. In other words he is obliging us actually to tell him what to program into the machine in his own terms.

When in later discussion members of the group tackled this problem directly by claiming that there was something called 'mystical experience' which existed beyond human language, and was therefore incapable of being defined, then the speaker simply refused to acknowledge its existence.

As mentioned earlier this form of argument can be modelled in terms of an extra dimension. The speaker defines his world in terms of pure mechanism. His opponent claims that the world thus defined is not the entire world: to prove this he has to provide examples of things that lie outside the world of mechanism. But, unless the speaker is himself able to or prepared to step outside the world of mechanism, his opponent is forced to describe his examples in terms that lie within the world of mechanism. Some of his examples can successfully be explained in such terms - those ones can now be dismissed because they have been shown to lie within the world of mechanism. Other examples defy all attempts to describe them mechanistically, for this reason the speaker insists that they 'do not exist'.

To his opponent the speaker seems like an inhabitant of 'Flatland', a two-dimensional world. He refuses to believe in a third dimension because he always demands to be shown it *within* his two dimensional world. If, say, his opponent attempts to demonstrate some 'miracle', such as converting a right handed glove into a left handed glove by flipping it over in the third dimension, he finds that the Flatlander has simply redefined a glove as an object that 'comes in two states and is capable of transformation between those states by some as yet unexplained mechanism'.

Another analogy is to consider someone who argues that there is no such thing as the 'Tao'. Most introductory taoist texts begin by saying that there is no exact equivalent of the chinese word 'tao' in English. So, what is it? Arthur Waley translates it as 'the way' - does that now mean there is an English equivalent? No, the Chinese concept means more than just 'the way'. What more does it mean?... The questioner will ask again and again for an explanation in English: each time he gets it he will claim that, if the explanation is correct, the tao must be a concept graspable in English. When told that the explanation is incomplete he will repeatedly ask what is missing. What he is saying is this: 'you keep telling me that there is a concept missing from the English language, but you don't seem able to explain what it is!'. Even if the questioner realises the paradox in his protest, and decides to learn all the world's languages in order to have the Tao explained to him, he still cannot succeed. This is because the key phrase in the Tao Teh King is that 'The Tao which can be described is not the true Tao', ie the Tao is itself a concept which lies beyond language.

This is the real difficulty for the machine intelligence advocate: a concept which lies beyond any language is a concept which could never be programmed, because there would be no language in which to program it. So either the concept does not 'exist', or else there is a limit to our ability to reproduce human consciousness by artificial means. The fact that those concepts which most inspire mankind are precisely those which do not 'exist' in these terms, is the reason why a programmable consciousness seems so claustrophobic and boring. (However, later in my story I try to show how such concepts might grow as a process within the system, and therefore not need to be programmable or describable as such - if it takes ten lifetimes to attain the Tao, then those ten lifetimes may add up to a description of the Tao, and 'beyond language' may turn out simply to mean 'beyond what any human could say in one lifetime'.)

Is the mystic's ineffable experience of the infinite no more than a refinement of the feeling that a computer has when bad programming causes it to try to divide some quantity by zero? I do not believe there is yet a simple answer to that question. What I am concerned to show is that the speaker had done no more in this argument than to counter my initial instinctive rejection of machine intelligence. Whereas I had thought 'of course a machine cannot think like a human, because it is only a machine', he had stated 'of course a machine can reproduce human thinking, because human thinking is only the working of a machine'. Whereas I had begged the question by assuming that machines by definition cannot think, he had begged the question by assuming that everything in our world was mechanical in the first place.

At that stage the discussion ended. The speaker had strengthened his position by giving a very good speech, one which took care of some of the more trivial objections to the idea of machine intelligence. On the other hand he had reached an impasse in the form of those of us who insisted there was something called 'mystical' experience, even though we could not define it to his satisfaction.

Why then did some of us feel threatened by his ideas?

An over-enthusiastic advocate of machine intelligence would have a simple answer to that question: we feel threatened because we are stubborn human beings and it hurts our pride to be compared to machines. This argument used to be put very forcibly when artificial intelligence was a novel idea being defended by 'angry young men': it makes a belittling assumption about the psychology of the non-believer, and therefore tends to betray strong conflicts in the feelings of those who state it most forcibly - like the adolescent children of pacifists, who love to lecture their parents on the subject of natural aggressive instincts. Genuine self esteem is not as vulnerable as this argument suggests: true, it would diminish us a bit to know that a human mind could be created without divine intervention, but we would at the same time feel pride at having achieved something that previous generations thought only God could do. The real threat lies not in hurt pride, but in a sense of spiritual claustrophobia.

His argument was a threat because it made our world smaller. By denying a dimension that lay outside the world of mechanism, it left us with a smaller world. Any idea that shrinks rather than expands my world is an act of violence to my spiritual claustrophobia, and is therefore 'bad'. Most people have a map of their universe that contains two areas: an area that is known, explicable, mechanical and predictable, and an area beyond it which contains all mystery. All the transcendent human qualities which we would not expect to be artificially creatable lie in this second area: so how do we react to the suggestion of artificial intelligence? Do we rejoice in the sudden expansion of the mechanical area to embrace the mystical area? Or do we deduce that the mystical area was a non-existent delusion? Most people seem to assume the second conclusion: they feel that artificial intelligence means a shrinking of our world to the exclusion of mystery. For some reason it is hard to separate the advance of technology from a process of reductionism - we become 'nothing but' machines.

Elsewhere[6] I have argued that all ideas, if accepted too universally, will tend to cramp our universe. The process is as follows. At a certain moment mankind is suffering from spiritual claustrophobia, then a new idea or way of thinking 'comes along' and it promises to expand the world and liberate us. It does this so succesfully that mankind ends up becoming the slave to the new idea, needing to be liberated once again. Christianity came like a beacon of hope into a world regimented by the Roman system; it liberated mankind, and later enslaved it. Science rescued mankind from the regimentation that the christian church enforced on our world, only to put us in another prison. The argument which suggested that there was nothing outside the mechanical universe was a threat because it was an argument that finally closed those prison gates.

That is what I see as the real threat: not just 'poor old mankind doesn't want to be taken off its pedestal', but rather the general observation that any idea that shows signs of diminishing the universe is an idea that needs to be transcended. It is a sign that a particular way of thought is growing senile. Reductionism is not fundamental to any world view: it is a demon which we conjure ourselves when we need to outgrow any theory. It forces us to rebel by creating spiritual claustrophobia, but do we still need such a drastic cure?

Elsewhere[7] I have argued for an alternative solution that challenges the reductionist demon itself. Instead of deducing that we are 'nothing but' machines, let us increase the mechanical world to embrace mystery. The idea of a computer which suffers from a nervous breakdown, or a robot which becomes a born-again christian, does not threaten us - it amuses us. It does so because it suggests machines growing into areas of unpredictability and craziness that were once beyond their reach - machines becoming 'unmechanical'. But the idea of a computer program which could precisely predict your next nervous breakdown would be a threat, because it would reduce that area of craziness into mechanical predictability.

If I create a machine that can full-bloodedly suffer the agonies of falling in love, then I have done something wonderful: I have revealed 'soul' in the motions of matter. If consciousness is totally the by-product of chemical reactions, then the rudiments of consciousness lie all about us: I can once more say that a flower turns towards the sun because it 'loves' the sun. The universe is now a living being.

If, however, someone else chooses to take the same evidence to prove instead that love is 'nothing but a chemical reaction', then I feel sorry for that person in his smaller world. May this book offer healing.

That explanation does something to suggest why the idea of machine intelligence was seen as a threat, but it does not fully explain the magnitude of the threat. After all, the evening had not ended with total defeat, but merely an impasse: some people were still acknowledging worlds beyond mechanism.

But it was not just the conclusions that were threatening, it was the way that they were presented.

Earlier I referred to our joke about the mechanical perfection of the speaker's performance on that evening. I then pointed out that the speaker was thereby 'living out the truth' of his own thesis. This was disturbing. To give a mechanically perfect argument in favour of mechanism is as unfair as it would be to make a romantically captivating speech in favour of romanticism!

What he had done was not just to present a good argument for machine intelligence, but also to realise the truth of his viewpoint by creating an argument that was itself mechanical. Although he never pointed out as much, and may not have done it deliberately, he was demonstrating a mechanism for defending machine intelligence. The mechanism was simply this: challenge the opponent to find something the machine cannot do; if he can define it exactly then build it into the machine by using his exact description; if he cannot define it exactly then ignore it and repeat the challenge. Such a mechanism is like a giant snowball in that it gathers momentum. It is a machine argument, because it runs to a clearly defined formula, and yet it can punch huge holes in the opposition to machine argument. In other words it is an algorithm for establishing the reality of machine intelligence.

On that occasion I could not understand what was happening in those terms.

But I could sense unconsciously that the speaker had created the argumentative equivalent of a tank; that early attempts to stop it were as ineffective as throwing stones at a tank; and that the final impasse reached was merely that some people had taken to throwing handfuls of air at the tank, and were consoling themselves that the tank could do no damage to the air they had thrown.

That was the threat which we sensed. Here was an idea that was dangerous because it could diminish the universe that we experienced, and it was being presented in a powerful way because the speaker's presentation was a living demonstration of the very point that he was trying to make.

Although the machine was still only within the speaker's mind, we had had our first argument with a machine, and had only managed to achieve a draw.

No wonder we felt threatened.

The Minister For Technology and The Pope - 3

Shattering. Utterly shattering.

The Pope glanced at the Minister for Technology. He too looked dazed - that was somehow reassuring. The Pope stretched and examined his hands, as if to reassure himself that they were real. Perhaps the most startling aspect of it all was to have been through such a shattering experience, and yet to have remained oneself... unshattered.

That was the problem. It all began to seem unreal. The experience of living through the Big Bang at the creation of a universe was simply more than the human mind could grasp. Even at the time its very vividness had a surreal, dreamlike quality. Again and again they had been forced to further 'dematerialise' from the experienced universe in order to reduce sensory overload. He removed the scanner helmet, turned to his companion, and shook him by the arm.

"This isn't going to work, you know. You can blow my mind a hundred times over with cosmic firework displays, but it won't convince me. God speaks to me most clearly in times of solitary communion, in subtle moments and in fine details. Do you understand?

"We have just witnessed a whirlwind ride through several million years of creation. At that sort of timescale you will stun me, but never convince me. I need to enter in, and live in this other reality. Not be whisked through it."

"I have already explained that." Without his customary impatient tone, John sounded a little crazy. He was emerging from shock towards a dizzy elation, a sense that he had done something, created something that put him on a level with God.

"I have explained that the initial stages of the program will run at breakneck speed and that it will progressively slow down as the inner universe grows increasingly structured. By the time intelligent life is forming the interreactions become so complex that the relative timescales will be rather more comprehensible: we will be able to cross them more easily, like a dream which spans a day yet happens in seconds. You'll be able to wander around for apparent days on end, savouring every second of it.

"But for now..." he rubbed his eyes and stretched "fifty million years is about enough for one day!"

That night, on the roof of his caravan, the Pope was fitful in his prayers. Every time he raised his eyes to the starlit heavens he felt an icy chill. God was present, but silent.

The Pope and the Minister for Technology, two spectres, stood side by side on the arid shore and watched a soggy sun set beyond a sultry sea. A riot of crimson created, according to John, by an unbreathable atmosphere thick with volcanic dust.

"This is the one. Definitely."

"But it's so... dead. Inhospitable. It's cruel."

"All my tests confirm that this planet has exactly the right conditions for life to evolve. Even better than our own one had."

"You know, JS, this isn't going to work. Ok, you've amazed me, but you've missed the real point. Look."

The Pope bent over and plunged his arm deep into a boulder. "This world is just a ghost. I can't touch it."

John laughed. "It's we *who are the ghosts! And you can learn to touch it once you begin to accept the evidence of your own ghost senses. My lads have done a lot of experiments on prototype 'inner worlds', and they find it's a knack, a combination of acceptance plus willpower. Have you never had a lucid dream? It's the same skill.*

"Realise that your whole being is now part of a larger program, the one program that embraces all manifestation. Your sense of isolation from the whole is itself part of that program, an illusion called self consciousness. Transcend it, but only as much as you need to become effective."

"Can you show me?" the Pope was prodding at a pebble with one finger, and thinking that John would make a great preacher.

"I haven't tried myself, and I have no intention of doing so. This is important. Remember, this is the last time I, or anyone else, comes with you into this universe. From now on it's all yours, because I don't want there to be any question in your mind that other people might be entering this universe in order to tamper with it, or create phenomena in order to fool you. From now on you are alone with the laws of physics.

"I, John Stephens, Minister for Technology of the realm, am giving you a universe!"

Glancing up, startled by the exultant cry, the Pope had a glimpse of hell, of diabolic triumph in John's eyes and was horrified.

The pebble shifted slightly.

The Pope gazed dejectedly at a small worm wriggling in the slime of a rock pool. He could strike out with his fist and pass like a ghost right through the worm without its even flinching. Yet again, a certain sort of concentration and the worm would suddenly freeze as his hand approached, sensing his presence.

Such experiments were no relief today. He had seen life create itself.

Recently he had begun to be ensnared by an old heresy, seeing the world as a creation of the Devil: an evil to be transcended by divine intervention. But John had shown him how to access the lower level software on Macroc. This meant that each time the Pope witnessed something that looked like divine intervention, something that seemed to transcend the laws of physics, he was able to re-run the principle of that event from memory, and Macroc would patiently illustrate how it had all happened as a consequence of chance interactions from the initial conditions.

The Pope fingered the magnetic card on the chain around his neck: the card that gave him exclusive access at any time to the Interface Chamber. He chose to take its image with him into this universe as a precaution. John always advised entering with some tangible reminder, ideally an unfamiliar physical defect or abnormality, something to ensure that one's experience of the other world was not too seductively real. Early researchers had lost their minds. The Pope chose not to enter as a giant or a cripple. Instead he bore this token on its unbreakable chain.

One little worm wriggled before him. A miracle, yet rather revolting. Like a maggot. From now on he was a pioneer. No previous computer had had the power to go beyond this point. The equations became too complex, memories had overloaded and partial solutions been resorted to. No previous explorer of inner space had seen more than this, experienced an artificial reality as complete as this, in all its detail.

The Pope had noticed the change in John. There was always something of the adolescent in him, a sneering know-all teenage kid. But this morning his 'I told you so' attitude was softened. He had seemed genuinely fascinated to hear about the Pope's inner experiences and discoveries.

"That worm is just a machine. It isn't alive" the Pope said to the empty beach. Pointlessly.

Pointlessly the Pope stood on the roof of his caravan and repeated his plea in a whisper to the starry sky. "Please tell me, Lord, am I right to go on with this?"

But he remained alone on the roof shrine of his caravan. God seemed to shun him. It was as if he had become infected, untouchable. The only answer came from logic - logic seemed to have all the answers nowadays. Logic reminded him that God had urged him into this quest, that God was omniscient, so God must be satisfied with the outcome.

Bloody logic.

"John? Can you lend me a cigarette?"

"Popes don't smoke!"

"At five o'clock this morning cigarettes were finally sanctified by papal decree."

John offered the cigarette without a smile. He too had been suffering loss of sleep. He was puzzled.

Observing the change in the Pope in recent days had evoked an unfamiliar feeling: the feeling of guilt. Where guilt had touched him there came a host of strange notions, rising like phantoms from his depths. He urgently wanted to run a Personality Profile Analysis of himself, but had missed his chance now the Pope had sole access to Macroc. John was sure that only Macroc could be trusted to analyse a mind as deep and sensitive as his own.

His motives had come into question. He had been so sure that it was all in the name of progress, to tighten up government by focussing power on the state and away from primitive superstition. And he favoured the tetrahedral form of government over the the present pyramidal one, because its extended symmetries would serve to restrain tyranny.

But he had begun to be aware of embarrassing personal interests. Among the Prime Ministers, he alone did not have a special title by tradition; he was branded with the 'minister for...' formula just like any junior minister. And the others knew it and made him feel like an upstart. His enviable popularity stemmed only from his position as provider of novelties for the masses. Similarly on the Council, despite smooth reassurances, he knew that he was expected to produce technological miracles to serve other ministers, rather than to serve the advance of technology itself. Like Macroc: mankind's ultimate triumph merely being handed over to the warlords.

John was half aware of his ambiguous motives. In condoning the idea that we were fighting an enemy unhampered by religious beliefs, he knew he had lied. Hadn't he seen evidence of some curious practices by the so-called enemy? Hadn't he long sensed in them just that element of unpredictability that worried him in the Pope... and in the masses. He suspected they were no less religious than ourselves, and that the warlords had simply been indulging in a little self deception to justify their own defeats. The very idea of a 'godless foe' was probably created from a desire to mobilise the masses. Politics internalised and running wild.

Along with this half-conscious scepticism, John had found a deeper doubt. He realised last night that he had never really believed in the enemy threat at all. A potential ally was being ritually slaughtered to keep a crumbling kingdom from disintegrating. A childhood memory returned: horror at seeing a priest blessing a tank. John had suddenly seen that he was not primarily at war with the Pope: conquering God was merely a strategic move fuelled by deep wells of anger, and initiated by a forgotten conviction that without religion man would have no Devil, and would never therefore go to war.

Each revelation offered temporary clarity, only to be confused by further discoveries about himself. Last night he had lain awake and pondered memories of his first love deciding, in the face of commitment, to leave him and become a nun. And of a nursery school teacher beating him hysterically because he had dared to experiment with the sun's rays and a magnifying glass - burning his initials on the sacred pages of a prayer book!

John saw himself as a model of reasonableness, an upholder of peace, yet others described him as a fighter. If he finally defeated the Pope, could he live without the struggle?

Reaching out to the Pope, John squeezed his arm and asked him how he felt.

"A few hours ago I was on this grassy slope, watching this sort of... ape. Do you know what it was doing? It was banging one stone against another, on and on like a stupid machine.

"Then it caught a spark. And it made fire.

"Yes, it knew what it was doing."

John wanted to jump up and shout 'I told you so', but this was not the occasion. Instead he put his arm around the Pope's shoulders and explained that they were making good time, and that it was possible to put Macroc on 'hold' for a day to allow them to rest and assimilate the experience.

The Pope shook his head. John offered to break his pact and be with him next time he entered the Interface Chamber. John was jumping for a chance to run that Analysis Profile. The Pope declined.

"So you really are ready for the next phase?"

The Pope nodded.

"You are prepared to re-enter that universe interactively, to speak with its inhabitants and give them the ultimate test: to see if you can in any way distinguish them from real human beings?"

"Unless I do it, what's the point?"

"Ok. But remember, there are two ways to do it. Each has its advantages, and its dangers. One is to go as you have always gone, as a 'ghost', but to 'materialise' more completely. Then you really would need more than just that card around your neck. Would an angel's wings and nightshirt really be so undignified? The best protective masks are the familiar yet ludicrous ones, apparently.

"The other way, one I would strongly recommend, is to take over a mind by 'possession'..."

"No!" The Pope protested angrily. "That ape. It wasn't the fire making. It was what happened next. Another one came out of the cave. One with..." the Pope made a gesture " you know... tits. And it was carrying a baby. And then the first ape ever so carefully picked up its little bundle of smouldering tinder... And he held it out towards them... And the look in his eyes... Oh God, I have never seen such... tenderness."

The Pope buried his head in his arms as if to weep, shuddered, then looked up again at John.

"It isn't like... evil" said John, surprised by his own choice of words. "Researchers in this field have found that it's like a surgical transplant: a mind can reject another one if it has to. Unless you really resort to extreme psychological violence, you can only get into a mind that is very much in tune with your own self. Even then it has to sort of... invite you. One of my lads said it can only be described as a 'partnership'.

"And it's the only way you will get what you really want: namely communication. If you appear as a ghost or angel you will have more trouble choosing your words. Looking back, you will never know how much the answers were affected by your own alien presence. Don't do it that way."

The shepherd shaded his eyes against the sun and watched the youth striding away down the track. Reaching the bend he stopped, looked back, and flung his arms out wide in a final farewell salute - then was gone.

"Strange lad that" said the shepherd to himself. "Got the makings of a priest".

The lad had admitted as much, a fascination for the priesthood that had little chance of recognition in a wandering cowherd.

A solitary type: he'd left his tribe to spend a few days in the mountains, but it hadn't made him any less friendly to the shepherd.

And good company. All those questions, and that funny way of his: half the time as serene and knowing as an elder, the other half all wide-eyed in childish wonder about the commonest things.

The shepherd wouldn't forget him in a hurry. At times he'd felt it wasn't healthy for a young lad to be asking about all those... peculiar things. Things he'd never thought much about himself, except perhaps alone in high places.

You couldn't forget those sort of conversations. They... changed you.

Good looking. He did once ask the lad if he would play the woman for him. Quite normal in the hills. The lad just said no with his funny smile, like he knew all about everything and just wanted to stay friends.

He would miss that lad.

The Pope already missed the body of a 17 year old cowherd. The return took some getting used to. He did not know how many minutes of real time he had been out, but he had lived three weeks in that time, wandered far and wide, and made many friends. He nursed his swollen shin: the result of forgetfully attempting a sprightly leap into his caravan.

At first the test itself had been almost impossible: that sense of trying to pull the puppet strings, and the slow discovery that it was more a question of a blending of wills. Superb training for marriage, perhaps?. Conversation always remained the most difficult thing: the hazy sense that you used to know all sorts of delicate concepts and clever words to convey meaning, and now all you knew was the language of an agricultural tribe. Yet the essence came through.

For a while he had doubted the very validity of the test itself. Is it not perhaps possible, he had thought, for a lifeless machine to imitate in every perfect detail the processes of a living being, yet to have no soul or self consciousness within?

And yet he knew that each one of us had already committed ourselves to the negative answer. Every little baby faces that dilemma when it begins to notice that other beings show signs of having some inner spark of consciousness in common with themselves. Every thinking child has at some time wondered if he alone is a living being, in a world of masked automata. The decision that all those other human beings have souls just like oneself is already made in childhood, and would not be overthrown in this lifetime.

Lying on his bed, smoking, the Pope now faced the aftermath. It was terrible.

He had spoken to John. John had been awfully nice about it, saying he wouldn't hold him to the official press conference and all that. But it was too late now really. Tomorrow it would all be over.

He would normally be in meditation at this time, rather than lying on his bed chain smoking. It simply wasn't done for a Pope to lie on his bed chain smoking. Which was one reason that he had chosen to lie on his bed chain smoking. He found value in being unpredictable.

'Do I feel guilty about lying on my bed chain smoking?' he wondered. 'No but I do feel bad about skipping the Benediction of the Sick.' He sighed at the terrible badness he felt at skipping the Benediction of the Sick. Real time spent within Macroc was actually so short, that he hardly had to alter his schedule on that account. It was the need to withdraw and ponder the changes in himself that had caused him to miss the Benediction of the Sick.

'I'm so glad I feel bad at missing the Benediction of the Sick', he thought, 'at least my conscience still shows signs of life. You have to be very careful with conscience, it's a sheep whose clothing fits the Devil all too well'. Although the Pope did not feel bad about lying on his bed chain smoking, he did feel bad about knowing why it was 'not done'. That implied lack of innocence.

An inner voice had told him that the death of the church was nigh, and that this would cast millions of ordinary folk into despair, deprive them of their hope, support and inspiration. In those circumstances the action of a real Pope would not be to wallow in hours of morbid introspection, but rather to devote every minute to preparing some comfort and guidance to the millions who were about to have their foundations knocked from under them.

The temptation was almost overwhelming, because the Pope knew that turning attention away from his own problems and back to his flock would be a certain way to reduce his own problems. It would also earn him greater honour at Court. Instead he chose the harder path, and lay on his bed chain smoking.

He owed his position to his early years spent championing the masses, fighting poverty, corruption, exploitation and disease. He had been swept into the Papacy as a hero, a Messiah. Then God had asked him to do the most difficult thing of all in his case: to turn inward in contemplation. Doing so had cost him political favour in high places, but not elsewhere. The masses had cried out for a hero, and God had given them what they actually needed - a mystery.

'If this had been a kingdom full of introverted mystics,' thought the Pope, 'I should now respond by playing the political activist. As it is, I will lie on my bed and face the Dark Night of the Soul, with another cigarette.'

He had gone up earlier and, of all things, apologised to God for no longer believing in Him. "But it isn't You I'm sorry for" he'd said "it's all those poor simple folk who are about to lose their religion. After all you're, were... would be omnipotent".

He blushed at the memory. But it was infinitely preferable to that other memory: the memory of conversations in that artificial world and his growing horror at hearing folk, all sorts of folk, simple ones, wise ones, clever ones, crooked ones, all talking about religion and God when he could sense, he actually knew, God wasn't there.

That universe was a cursed spawn of the devil. A godless vacuum. He had fled back to this world to find now that God was dead here too.

Or was he?

Suddenly the Pope sat up. A jab of pain from his shin, but he grabbed his coat.

The vast oak door closed with a thud. The Pope listened to the dying echo before running forward crying ecstatically "Howdy Lawd! Ah's a-comin' HOME!"

Freezing in his flight, he followed the echo of his cry up into the gilded darknesses of soaring vaults and the intricate traceries of endless far chapels.

Silliness. He felt that the Minister for Technology had lured him into eating of the Tree of Knowledge and he had been cast into outer darkness as a consequence. One should not automatically despise silliness. One should not automatically despise anything. All automatism reduced one to a machine. Silliness was hope. Trying to get back to that youthful innocence.

He didn't care if the cardinals heard that. They were already a little shaken by a midnight visit from His Holiness, demanding the key to the Cathedral. The papal guard were totally thrown by the sudden nocturnal resumption of formalities.

He was approaching the High Altar.

On the death of his father he had decided to leave the Papal Palace and adopt a nomadic life. One consolation of a decline in favour at Court was that it made it easier for a Prime Minister to indulge his eccentricities. He had begun to know a different face of God: that experienced by the Desert Messiah, the Wanderer in the Waste. He had never felt closer to Him than on the roof of his little caravan. Until now.

So he had returned to base camp.

The Pope knelt at the high Altar and began to pray in earnest.

Three hours and a stiff, pain wracked body later he was locking the great door once more behind him. The key was heavy bronze: wielded it could kill a man.

In that time he had had only one inspiration, an inspiration for a great service: the Cathedral plunged into darkness, thunderous organ music rising, rising to a fearful crescendo then, BLAM, two crossed spotlights - in harsh arc-light white - knife down from the heavens onto the sole figure of His Holiness the Pope in purest white silk robes. He flings wide his arms and screams into the darkness "MY GOD! MY GOD! WHY HAST THOU FORSAKEN ME!"

What theatre! Relayed by satellite television all over the globe - what a parting gift to his beloved flock!

But what potential for an ego trip into kitsch. He would have to work on it.

Now God was dead. And now, curiously, there was only one place where the Pope felt welcome. The key to that place was as light as a feather on the chain around his neck. And there was time to kill.

3
In Defence of Artifical Intelligence

IN THIS CHAPTER I argue for the possibility of artificial intelligence in its fullest sense. If I see the concept as a threat, why argue in its defence? The normal reaction of those who are threatened is to deny that true intelligence could ever be produced artificially.

The original impetus for writing this book was in order to help pay my mortgage. Imagine yourself in the same position, choosing a subject for a book that is likely to sell. Let us imagine that you choose to write a book on the horrors of naziism - a topic that sells fairly readily.

There is plenty of evidence of the nasty things done in the name of naziism, all good material for a book. But the biggest horror lies in the fact that the story is so close to home: it does not concern savages in some bygone age, but people of an advanced Western civilisation, people not very different from ourselves. So your book would have much more impact if, instead of just listing the nasty things that nazis did, you wrote something about the doctrines of naziism, about the very high ideals that it tried to realise, and about the positive stimulus it also gave to a nation. For the full danger can only be appreciated when your readers understand some of the temptations that made many otherwise sensible and basically well-meaning people support the nazi movement.

The better you present the case for naziism as it then seemed, the more powerful, thought provoking, and potentially valuable would be your book. And the better chance of it paying your mortgage. But only as long as people don't think the book is meant primarily to be a defence of naziism.

The last chapter was about the threat posed by artificial intelligence. I believe many people have sensed that threat, but not many non-specialists have had the time or inclination to think it through as thoroughly as myself. Some have responded by dismissing the idea too hastily, finding one over-simple argument against artificial intelligence and using it as a shield. This is a precarious way to resist a threat, and this book could do a lot to reassure such people, but only if they can face the possibility of its predictions.

This chapter attempts to justify artificial intelligence, because the rest of the book will be much more interesting if readers see my thesis as being based upon a real possibility. But I would hate you to judge the book by this chapter, and would hate you to see the book as an attempt to justify or 'prove' artificial intelligence, a subject about which I have very little specialist knowledge.

Instead of trying to present a coherent reasoned case in its favour, I will look at some of the over-simple arguments used to oppose artificial intelligence, and explain why I find them inadequate.

'You can only get out what you put in'

I have often heard this argument: no machine could ever be creative, because it can only do what some human has programmed it to do.

The persistence of this argument is surprising. Perhaps it is because it has some Truth; however this only goes to show how inadequate Truth is as a sole measure of merit.

Consider the most recent chess-playing programs. I gather that they can present quite a challenge to human chess masters, even if they cannot yet humiliate them. But does that mean that the people who wrote the programs must also be chess masters? I am sure there must be programs that can play better chess than the people who wrote the programs.

I have occasionally played chess, but have never studied it. If asked to create a chess playing program I might proceed as follows.

First the rules of chess are programmed, then a random move generator is created using the random number command. That means we now have a device that will always play by the rules, but will play totally at random with no tactics.

Next we provide it with a memory of previous games, and an ability to scan that memory.

Next we program an ability to recognise situations. This is the tricky part: an enormous amount of time and memory could be saved if we did this cleverly, so that the machine could recognise what the significant elements of a pattern were, and concentrate on those. However, let us be simple and clumsy: our machine will be too stupid to recognise abstract patterns, it will only recognise if it has been in this precise situation before; and it will remember whether the move it then made lead to a win or a defeat.

At this point it is tempting to program the machine to always repeat its previous winning moves. However that could restrict its 'learning' into closed loops, it might just repeat the same game over and over again without discovering an even better move. Instead we 'weight' the random move generator so that the machine is much more likely (rather than absolutely certain) to make the winning moves, and much less likely to make the losing moves.

Finally we set the machine to play endless games against itself - several games at once if possible.

This program as described is, no doubt, an absolute monstrosity, a hydrogen bomb to peel a grape. It would demand the most colossal computer memory (unless we were clever about programming in an ability to recognise abstract patterns) and it would run painfully slowly. But, in theory, it would eventually play chess better than I can, simply because it very seldom makes the same mistake twice, and therefore learns by experience.

There is truth in the statement that you can only get out what you have put in, though it does not stop a nurseryman from planting acorns; but what if you have put in an ability to remember and learn, as in the above example?

When the 'you can only get out what you put in' argument is presented against artificial intelligence it seems to assume the following: that the programmer is claiming to be able to study a human being then write a program which, when fed into a computer, will cause it to display every sign of human intelligence. This is surely an unrealistically advanced idea? I would be surprised if anyone could even write a champion chess program that would win its very first game, for I suspect that most such programs depend upon some measure of learning by experience.

Take a very clever learning device, yourself for instance. How much easier is it to learn a foreign language by living in the foreign land and using the language, than by sitting in a classroom back in England? Which would be the easier way to educate an intelligent baby, by confining it to a sensory deprivation environment and getting the world's best teachers to spend all day telling it about the world; or by letting it live a normal life within the world?

So what would be the easier way to program a rather less brilliant machine? Surely the easiest route would be to give it senses, a memory and an urge to explore?

I accept that a human mind might be so complex that no human programmer could ever create one from first principles. However I believe it might be possible for a human to invoke a human mind. This is a much less deterministic ambition, and it might be realised by transmitting the sensory input of a human body (as digitised neural impulses) back to a base computer and returning signals to activate the body's muscles, then waiting to see what happens. The personality that developed would probably be as unpredictable as the personality of any child - it would be an invoked personality rather than a created personality.

You could argue that intelligence that is invoked cannot be called 'artificial' - 'arti' is ok, but not 'ficial' - but that is too fine a distinction for this book. Once we've built a gadget that can write this book better than I can, I'll be happy to call it 'artificial intelligence', however it was done.

Now, once something like a human mind has been invoked by any means, there is the intriguing possibility of transmitting its memory into other devices, and multiplying the mind. I can accept that a human mind is too complex to be formulated by any human programmer, but that does not stop us from doing it in stages, creating a machine sufficiently complex to be capable of designing an even more complex machine, and so on until something approaching human intelligence has been created.

The expert critic

I recall discussing this thesis with a computer buff twelve years ago. He had no faith in artificial intelligence because he argued that the animal brain is a parallel processing device, whereas a computer is not. To that I replied 'then we must build a parallel processing computer!'

How powerful is ignorance! It is rash statements like that which lead to the most spectacular successes. For I had little idea of what was meant by a parallel processor.

We are here trying to cope with not one, but a whole class of objections. They come from people who have, or affect to have, greater working knowledge of the technology than myself: they may be genuine experts, or they may be people who have just read an expert article which seemed to be stating that artificial intelligence was impossible. From that position of strength they point out that there is an undeniable practical reason why artificial intelligence is a hopeless proposition.

To that sort of argument I have two objections. One is a logical one: if it is definitely a hopeless quest, why are artificial intelligence projects still being funded by large institutions worldwide?

The other one is an intuitive extrapolation from those expert objections that I have already understood (let's forget the ones which went over my head). In those cases I have found that the 'insurmountable obstacle' is on inspection usually just a cul-de-sac from the main line of progress. To take my above example: I cannot conceive how anyone, even in the earliest days of research, could ever have expected to emulate human thought without running multiple functions in parallel. But apparently someone did try to do it; and no doubt they published a learned article explaining that the project had failed, 'because the brain is a parallel processor'.

Because there are a lot of researchers busy investigating what can be achieved within the limited scope of their particular project and funding, there are inevitably a lot of dead ends being explored. And plenty of learned articles coming out about the deadness of those ends. Whenever someone presents what is clearly an informed refutation, but one which concludes 'therefore artificial intelligence is a hopeless quest', rather than 'therefore artificial intelligence is still only a long term hope', then I suspect that the argument has used one of those articles for its inspiration, but the speaker's real motivation is the emotional sense of being threatened, as suggested earlier.

In other words: it is not enough to present a reasonable argument, it is still possible to be betrayed by the force of the conclusions you draw from it.

'Of course you've totally overlooked the negative entropy parameter'

Again we are dealing with a whole class of objections. Whereas the last objector was someone who had read a learned account of a failed project or wrong philosophical approach, and was drawing too global a conclusion from it, this objector is an a pompous ignoramus throwing up a smokescreen. Two examples from radio discussion programmes will illustrate.

One was about astrology: when an 'expert' was asked to comment he said astrology was bunk because astrologers said, for example, 'the Sun was in Cancer' when actually Cancer was a constellation of stars millions of miles distant, and the Sun was not 'in' it. Unfortunately for Common Sense, the programme's compere did not reply 'you stupid twit, when astronomers talk about the difficulty of optical observation of stars while the Sun is 'in' the sky, they don't surely believe it is floating in our atmosphere any more than the astrologers believe the Sun has shot away into the distant galaxy?'. Instead he said 'well, you have obviously studied this subject very deeply' - and he was not being sarcastic. Of course 'the Sun in Cancer' is a precisely defined astrological statement about the Sun's angular position relative to Earth, and it has nothing directly to do with the constellation called Cancer, because of the subsequent progression of the Equinoxes. Far from having studied the subject deeply, the expert made a fool of himself.

The other was a discussion about reincarnation. Someone had suggested the possibility that those who recalled past incarnations might somehow have tuned into 'disembodied information' about the past. This suggestion was instantly dismissed by another speaker, who said 'what nonsense! information is energy - it cannot possibly exist in any disembodied form!'. Unfortunately this was said in such an authoritative manner that the original idea was squashed. It seems that no-one present had done 'O' level physics, otherwise they would have realised that information is not energy ('today is Tuesday', 'today is not Tuesday' - two units of information which add up to zero information, thus proving information is not a scalar quantity, which energy definitely is).

In both cases the technique is to quell opposition by speaking the most absolute balls, but with the full weight of authoritative conviction. I cannot of course anticipate such objections here, all I can do is to point out that some people who feel threatened by artificial intelligence will throw up totally spurious objections which simply confuse the issue.

That the brain is fundamentally different from a computer

Certainly the brain is very different from any existing computer, but as long as people are capable of precisely describing what it is in the brain that makes it different from a computer, then that precise description is itself the recipe for the machine we must next create. As in the last example: if the brain is a parallel processor, then we must make a computer that is a parallel processor if we are to model the brain exactly.

I would certainly expect the technology to have changed considerably before we can mimic human thought. My picture of artificial intelligence has never been one of being able to buy 'human mind' software for your desktop computer. Silicon chips may never suffice: I suspect that the correct approach would mimic cellular growth itself, to produce a computer that is an organic culture rather like the grey matter of the brain itself. The more precisely we research the brain to discover what makes it different from present computers, the more precisely will we be able to reproduce its working. I gather that research is indeed being pursued along these lines.

The only other alternative is one that I find unlikely: it is one that might be expected in a mystical quest but not in a scientific quest. It is that there should be discovered some absolute limitation which defines an impassible abyss between the human mind and anything we can create.

Even if it is discovered that there is some special quality in the human organism which means that the only way the workings of the brain and nervous system could be duplicated was in their precise present form, why could one not reproduce that form as an organic culture *in vitro*?

That the brain is only the receiver, not the generator of mind

This is a rather different type of objection, one that I find much more interesting and unanswerable. It recognises that thought does seem closely linked to the brain, but suggests that we are wrong to assume therefore that 'mind' is generated by the brain in the way a computer generates its calculations. Perhaps mind exists as immaterial 'spirit' which needs a brain only to focus it, rather as wireless waves need a radio set to make themselves manifest.

If that is your fundamental objection to artificial intelligence, I will not attempt to counter it. Instead I beg you to be patient with the book and to read on, because you will find that later chapters cast some interesting light on the possibility of disembodied intelligence, supporting your idea at its weakest point - namely, how could thought exist without a material foundation?

That we do not need artificial intelligence

Don't laugh, but I have heard it said by an apparent expert that we will not develop machines to think like humans because we do not need machines which think like humans.

This will be tackled more thoroughly later when I discuss creativity, Chapter 7, but here I will simply point out that we do not need governments, we do not need nuclear weapons, we do not need soap operas on television... indeed, the less something is needed the more effort mankind is likely to put into it.

'Amdahl and the Ant'

This is an argument which begins as follows: you cannot deny the enormous progress made in computers - the Amdahl supercomputers can perform calculations which would take a man a lifetime - but we have utterly failed to imitate so much as the intelligence of an ant.

Whereas the 'expert' argument was a qualitative one, this is a quantitative one. The former picks on some specific quality of mind which we have not matched, this argument ignores individual qualities and directs attention to the magnitude of the gulf we have failed to cross: a multi-million pound development has not even achieved the intelligence of a tapeworm, let alone a human.

To me this argument shows the extraordinary short-sightedness that our scientific education has fostered. We have created plenty of machines more intelligent than a tapeworm, the point is that it has not been done by the artificial intelligence experts. As is so common in life, we succeed best when not trying too hard. But such is our shortsightedness that, when I illustrate my point, people think I am being funny.

A bureaucracy, or any human institution, is a machine that shows signs of intelligence. People who cannot accept this fact are inclined to attribute the intelligence of the organisation to the humans within it, and develop a corresponding contempt for bureauocrats.

Give it a test: try to get something useful out of any civil service department through the official channels, and you will be thwarted at every stage by a mind which exhibits a low cunning geared to its own survival at the expense of all else. The same malignant parasitism can be found in any profession as an entity: the Law ever creates the conditions for its further growth and influence, so does Medicine as a profession look after its own welfare better than it looks after the health of the individual humans who feed it.

The civil service is a machine vastly more intelligent than a tapeworm - though I have to admit it does lack the warm humanity and lively wit of the latter - but the intelligence of the organism is totally the product of its structure and not a derivative of the human minds which partake in it. I have been a civil servant and would be the first to admit that civil servants can be quite nice, if you like that sort of thing. Elsewhere[8] I have described how the civil service has created a system which only allows one way out of any position: it is to be promoted. Any programmer would immediately recognise this as a neat 'sort' mechanism for ensuring that everyone ends up in the job they are bad at. Thus the system minimises the 'noise' of human individuality by ensuring that the whole organisation is made up of un-motivated paper pushers. Humans are reduced to logical gateways in the vast parallel processor which makes up the low mind of the civil service.

Consider the medical profession as another example. It has campaigned for a health warning to be printed on every packet of cigarettes. Everyone knows that health is strongly linked to psychological factors, and that if you repeatedly tell somone their health is suffering then they are likely to grow sick by suggestion - especially if this suggestion is implanted at times of tension, which is precisely when many people choose to take a cigarette. It would be better to present people with images of outdoor living, wild horses and rugged good health at these times, but these are exactly the images that have been banned from association with cigarettes. Thus the medical profession as an entity is securing itself by invoking sickness in society: another way it does this is by regularly announcing an ever changing list of the commonest foods as being particularly bad for health. Yet I defy anyone to find a single doctor who has deliberately set out with a policy of making people ill in order to increase their professional influence.

There is always a total distinction between the quality of the minds of the individuals in an organisation and the quality of the mind exhibited by the organisation itself - whether it be a profession, a union, a government, an army or whatever. The organisation will show signs of intelligence, and of personality, but it has nothing to do with the minds of the people in it. This mind is rather a phenomenon generated by the network of interactions within the organisation and its learned responses to outside stimuli. No doubt Darwinian selection plays its part here: a medical profession which made everyone healthy would die of its own success, and liberal governments are simply those that permit their own downfall.

What I am suggesting is that mankind has already made much greater progress in the creation of artificial intelligence than we realise, but that the progress has been made as a by-product of other enterprises rather than being made in the laboratories. Future progress in artificial intelligence will probably be fostered by an analysis of the rather more flexible and open structures of human organisations to see how they develop their intelligent responses.

Perhaps we will learn to see the Inland Revenue not as a gang of malignant human outcasts but rather as a tribal god to which one should offer burnt sacrifices? And if those sacrifices should just happen to take the form of the odd VAT Inspector, I for one will not hasten to protest.

'A subset cannot be a superset'

This is a philosophical problem. If artificial intelligence in its fullest sense is possible, it will mean the possibility of making an object which can think like a human. (To assume a half-way position and to say that intelligence will be created but it can never have the same quality as a human intelligence is to re-invoke the question 'why?' - why could it never be intelligent enough to find out the difference between its intelligence and ours, and therefore learn to emulate that difference?).

But a device which thinks just like a human would need to have the background knowledge of a human: it would have all the different inner 'maps' (as described in my introduction) that make up our image of the world. It would need all the memories of a lifetime. I can recall an enormous wealth of memories, but behind it all is a far vaster store of memories beyond direct recall. For example: I have no recollection of the dress that was worn by the woman in whose arms I ceased to be a virgin, but if anyone wanted to re-create that scene under laboratory conditions (any offers?) and they chose the wrong dress, I would very likely know it was wrong. Apparently one can demonstrate almost perfect recall of such incidents under hypnosis.

If one can map a mind with all its memories and knowledge of the world into a device, then one could make the device a bit larger and map the entire contents of *two* minds into it. Note that it would not need to be twice as large, because there would be a fair proportion of repeated knowledge. Make it a bit larger and it contains three minds, four minds, a hundred minds... the minds of the entire population of the earth. How big would it need to be? I would estimate that a cube the size of a football field could probably contain the sum total of all human brain matter on earth at present: but, allowing for the overlapping effect, you could presumably map all the minds into a much smaller cube. Double the result and you would have room not just for the minds of all humans alive today, but for all humans which have ever walked this earth.

Within that device the entire consciousness of humanity could be living in a sort of dream world which was indistinguishable from the reality of our universe.

This is where the objection comes: here is a cube which is but a tiny speck on the surface of a minor planet in an average solar system, but it is supposed to contain the sum total of all human knowledge - a knowledge that extends millions of light years into space. When we have found out everything about our planet earth, that 'tiny' cube will contain all of that information. It will be a relatively minute part of the earth's matter, but it will theoretically contain the whole earth and a lot of other experience within it in the form of coded information. How can a small part of something contain the whole thing and more? How can a subset of a set also be its superset?

This is an objection that I am compelled to recognise rather than just dismiss. It is too much of a diversion from the main point of this book to pursue at length. As a clue to my attitude on this subject I will make two observations.

The first is that we are touching on the problem of the microcosm and the macrocosm, a problem which has long intrigued mankind - the part which equals the whole.

Secondly I believe that time is the key. The whole of centuries of English literature is no more than permutations of 26 letters and a few punctuation marks. Putting them in sequence (ie ordering along a 'time' dimension) creates the literature. Those same letters in sequence could record the sum total of knowledge in the English language (we'd better forget the 'Tao' mentioned in the last chapter). But we are being too profligate: we only need two characters, namely the dot and dash of morse code to do that.

Take two states, the 0 and the 1 of a digital computer, add an extra dimension along which they can be ordered in sequence, and they can describe a whole universe. This identification of Time and Order with the birth of manifestation is quite appropriate to some of mankind's oldest spiritual traditions, so I will leave it merely as a suggestive response to this last objection to artificial intelligence, and return to the theme in Chapter 6 where it is presented as an example.

The Minister For Technology and The Pope - 4

TA TARA RATATA... The Pope followed the fanfare with his lips then winced into a rictus of pain as it cracked on the final chord. 'Royal ceremonial is rubbish nowadays' he thought. 'Back in the Papal Palace we always got it right. A man can't blow true without the love of God in his lungs. They'd have done penance for a week in the dungeons for that racket.'

He sensed a heavy atmosphere among the massed Ministers. 'They've killed God and, instead of rejoicing, they're wracked with guilt.'

Only the King looked happy, leaning over the arm of his golden throne and beaming as the enormous diamonds on the royal yo-yo flashed, spinning up and down, up and down. He played it straight, with the odd backhand flip. He couldn't quite manage a 'round the world loop' on this one, it was too heavy. It would be fatal to try it prematurely before the press.

The King drummed his heels against the jewelled throne and blew little bubbles of saliva in delight. He knew the importance of image before the press: his Minister for Technology had once run him a Quantitative Charisma Profile on one of those gadgets of his. And the press sounded a bit dangerous today.

The second fanfare was for the four Prime Ministers to converge and kiss each other before the image grab video cameras of the press - vital to be seen doing that in public. The Pope received, and responded to, the warm squelch of Mavis, the conquering swoop of Irma and then, as John's lips pecked his cheek, the Pope struck a dramatic pose and thought "betrayed with a kiss". John's hands remained on his shoulders, "are you ok?" he whispered.

"Yes, past the worst."

"Thank God for that." John turned away before the Pope could laugh in his face.

This was the Pope's day.The Minister for Technology gave the introduction, set the scene, and then the King pointed his sceptre at the Pope. The Pope confirmed the facts, and told his story to the press, who made notes in silence and ever held their videos at the ready - to trap any fleeting image which would convey it all to the masses.

Then the Minister for Technology thanked the Pope for his cooperation and expressed his condolences. He explained that Macroc was now free to serve the War Minister but, in an attempt to woo a sultry press, suggested that it be left available for inspection during the rest of the day, before being switched off and reprogrammed.

"Excuse me, your Majesty!" the Pope exclaimed, only to be silenced with a wave of the King's hand. As the King turned toward the War Minister he sensed a sullen ripple among the press. No-one who hoped to stay long on the

throne could afford to ignore that sound. In one skillful continuous movement the King deflected, and turned his sceptre back to the Pope.

"Your Majesty, the Minister for Technology has spoken of switching off Macroc. That cannot be done."

A baffled silence.

"It would destroy a universe, your Majesty."

Awkward instant, then the Minister for Technology stepped reassuringly forward. "If I may intervene, your Majesty?

"My friend and colleague has had a very disturbing few days. You must understand that, although he has witnessed nothing more than a program within a computer, it has had all the vividness of a real life experience. In consideration of mine own part in setting up this experiment, may I ask leave to beg your pardon for this interjection on his behalf?"

The King beamed, but dare not ignore the Pope's mounting agitation.

"Your Majesty, I committed myself to this experiment on the condition that it should be demonstrated that the products of a chance concurrence of the laws of physics would prove to be in no way distinguishable from the contents of our own universe. Now the Minister for Technology is himself recognising a very clear distinction.

"God died to me, but has now risen. I have found him well and living in the mind of the Minister for Technology, who believes that our 'chosen' people have a right to survive that is denied to those within Macroc. Unlike him I know, I have lived with the people within Macroc, and know that they too are God's children. Have you forgotten Henry the Twelth, your Majesty?"

The King winced, and sought some distant, elevated object upon which to fix the regal gaze. A more painful comparison could hardly have been made. As a youth he had met Henry, just before his death. Poor Henry had courted popularity by founding a wondrous charitable isolation hospital on a small offshore island. Then word had leaked out about a few, hopeless remnants of some dwindling but obstinate tribe that had been quietly, and most humanely 'removed' in order to hasten the project. The resulting character assassination in the press had left him only three weeks before he had chosen the Royal Prerogative, and retired to his bedchamber with his sword.

"This calls for further consideration" he said. A cue for hubbub, or so it seemed to the King. But Junior Ministers later described it as the most stimulating parliamentary debate within memory.

Irma's Generals rushed forward with the irrefutable evidence that we were about to be overrun by a vicious, all-powerful enemy whose only challenge lay in the immediate military re-deployment of Macroc. Meanwhile Mavis and her team of advisers produced precise statistics to explain why 'wasting' Macroc would spell instant economic ruin.

And yet, allowing of course for the need for a thorough investigation of the matter, the group decision was that the Pope had a valid point. For the time being, at least, Macroc would be left running.

If only the Pope hade left it at that. Unfortunately he seemed to have got the bit between his teeth.

"Your Majesty, you appear to have misunderstood the gravity of the situation. We cannot just leave it at that! Inside Macroc there are atrocities being committed! There is war, famine, plague, human despair! Have we lost all sense of responsibility to those under our care? Those we have actually created?"

The King made the mistake of attempting to exclude the Pope from further debate, which then took a rather curious turn as the Ministry for Technology team were now left in charge of a discussion about moral responsibility.

It started with an enthusiastic Master Programmer who came forward with an imaginative scheme whereby he could operate on the low level software of Macroc to gradually eliminate concepts of 'pain', 'evil' and so on from the inner universe. He was getting into top gear when a Scientific Correspondent reminded him that his signature was recorded on a petition to the King, protesting at the appointment of a doctor who had once proposed remedial brain surgery on pathological criminals. "And what's the difference? except that you *are proposing it on a whole universe?" came the punch line.*

A Social Anthropologist on secondment from the Ministry of Education added his criticism to such an insensitive approach. It was clear that education was the only ethical solution. It would be necessary to make contact with someone in a position of authority, the leader of the dominant tribe, and enlighten them as to the nature of their universe.

At that point someone interrupted to remind him that he had been one of the judicial advisers in a recent case where several of the Pope's missionaries had been gaoled for attempting to make converts among a hill tribe whose primitive religious beliefs came under the Protection of Endangered Ideologies Act. Would he please clarify his own position?

And so on, and on, and on. The signs of discontent in the public gallery were already showing when an adviser to the Minister for Health, a man with the diplomatic finesse of a berserker, suggested they put Macroc on 'hold' until a legalisation of euthanasia had been rushed through parliament and then... but the rest was drowned in a roar of disapproval. Euthanasia was this season's hate-topic.

The King lost his nerve. Noises from the galleries had taken their toll of his courage, and he desperately needed a few minutes to gather his wits. The only voice that had seemed capable of creating a deathly hush was that of the Pope. Perhaps if he permitted the Pope to speak? He was, after all, a decent sort of chap and, now he had seen the trouble he had caused, perhaps he might temper his views? Pointing the sceptre at the Pope, the King crossed his fingers and dared to hope for an extremely long winded and uncontroversial apology.

"Thank you, your Majesty.

"One thing has become very clear: the Ministry for Technology is ill-equipped to cope with this moral dilemma. As we have seen, the only certain course is to commit mass murder, and switch off Macroc. Apart from that, as has already become apparent, it is not possible to shift one single atom in that inner universe without initiating an endless chain of effects. And, as has already been explained, the only way to predict those effects would be to use Macroc. And the

only program that could do that with utter certainty is the one already running in Macroc, for this universe is a turbulent system.

"This poses a problem for people who admit no other authority than pure reason. Any decision they make might lead to some regrettable side-effect. The public would then hold them responsible for those consequences. So they dare not make any group decision.

"Here I have an advantage. For I can commune with God and be His mouthpiece, or I can act on my conscience. In either case the majority of the public will accept this, and judge the consequences of my decision by quite different criteria. One example will illustrate, and also point the way to a solution.

"Last night I must have spent a good thousand years inside Macroc, I was so appalled at the state of our creation. Do you know, I found one race - a whole race - in total subjection to another, serving as slaves and living under an genocidal edict that all their male children must be slaughtered at birth? One slave woman tried to hide her kid from this fate, but he was a little terror. I have known many families in my calling, and it is often easier for an outsider than for a parent to distinguish when a child is a problem because of too much rather than too little soul. This was one of those - there was no chance of hiding a kid like that.

"I had to remain an unseen observer while that mother made a little boat out of rushes, put the baby in it, and left it amongst the reeds by the river bank. What could I do? Materialise like a ghost and cause panic, and the certain death of them both? Then I saw a wealthy woman from the master race walking towards the spot - the sort of woman who would easily have the resources to look after an infant prodigy. And I did something that would never be justified by pure logic. I tossed a pebble into the water. The woman heard the splash and looked, then saw the baby in the boat. She took it and, God be thanked, loved it. Then I left Macroc on 'hold', because in our outer world it was time for this... event.

"As has already been suggested, it would be a mistake to try to influence a man of power in the inner world. Any knowledge we give him might be perverted to increase his own power. But, while others were arguing, God suggested to me a plan for leading that slave race - a people with nothing to lose - out of bondage and into isolation where they could be educated. A first step in a divine plan to redeem the universe within Macroc.

"Your Majesty, who but myself could be trusted with that responsibility?"

The King was quite entranced. Such a nice man the Pope, and no nasty noises from the gallery. In fact, there were signs that the public would take the plight of the poor Macroc-folk to heart, be delighted to find someone worse off than themselves! Associating positively with such a mission could only be good for the royal image!

"Why yes! How splendid!" the King cried.

Unfortunately however the Pope was not such a good politician. He went too far, and blew his advantage.

"In which case, your Majesty, with a whole Universe added to my flock, our church will be grossly under-resourced. I will therefore be forced to insist upon

a revoking of certain recent measures. I would ask for a reinstatement of grants to church schools, a de-secularisation of tithes, a restoration of the monasteries... "

Gasps of horror from Mavis awoke the King from his happy dream. His jaw dropped and he froze to his throne. Sensing a loss of advantage the Pope hastily added "...and of course we will also tighten our own belts." But it was too late. The King raised his sceptre, he needed a second opinion to do the dirty work, fast. Who was it to be?

Irma? She was on the point of blowing her top - too much the soldier, not enough the politician.

Mavis? Heavens no! Not with the press in this mood!

There was nothing for it, but the bastard who created this mess in the first place. At least he too was popular. Divide the masses and rule!

John found the sceptre pointing at himself, and was at a loss - had to say something. His mind was blank as he walked over to the Pope and laid a hand on his shoulder. "Your Majesty, His Holiness the Pope is absolutely right. We are privileged to be witnessing a turning point in man's philosophical and spiritual understanding. A meeting of technology and religion of such importance that temporary considerations of war and economy will soon be forgotten. Your Majesty's reign will make history!"

Bullshit or not, it went down like honey. John was politician enough to recognise the movement in the gallery and to square his shoulders and thrust his chin purposefully forward for his final words.

But he need not have bothered. The press made their own interpretation of events. The image they were grabbing was that of the sagging features of a defeated War Minister.

4
The Purpose of The Story

It is unusual to find a fictional story used as an illustration in a non-fiction book. In the introduction I compared this book to such other world-expanding books as *The Chariot of the Gods*. Such books tend to rely heavily on factual evidence, and probably avoid any suggestion of fiction, as though it might cast doubt on the rest of the book. But the trouble with factual evidence as a basis for a revolutionary idea is that it is so vulnerable: the more closely the evidence is followed up by a critical reader, the more doubtful it becomes. Once doubt sets in, such readers end up believing that the whole book is founded on fiction.

Perhaps in the present case, having started from a foundation of blatant fiction, the only direction this book can progress towards is that of greater truth: the more it is considered, the truer it will become. In a later chapter I return to the discussion of 'living' an idea, allowing it to grow in truth, as an advance upon merely 'understanding' it.

In the story, the Minister persuades the Pope to enter into a fiction world, and he does so in order to alter the Pope's belief about the real world. According to strict logic that should not happen: nothing that is proved in a fictional world need have any bearing on the real world. But the Minister knows that our thinking is not governed by logic alone; it is also governed by a principle of economy called 'Occam's Razor'. According to this principle, the human mind rightly prefers to limit the number of entities in its comprehension. In the ecology of the human mind, Occam's Razor results in a natural sceptical tendency that acts as a balance to, or restraint on, the equally natural tendency to phantasy.

To give an example of its working: when we see Uri Geller baffling scientists with a spoon bending feat, the phantasising tendency in us rejoices at the evidence of mysterious paranormal powers. But when, shortly after, we see a self-confessed conjuror like David Berglas baffling the same scientists with an apparently identical feat, then Occam's Razor makes us sceptical about Uri Geller. Because we now *know* these effects can be done by un-paranormal trickery, the principle of economy makes it hard for us to believe that there are also paranormal powers capable of producing the identical effect.

Of course, if strict logic was the only consideration, this would not follow: the fact that person A can imitate an effect by normal means does not exclude the possibility of B's having done it by paranormal means, any more than the fact that we can make diamonds in a laboratory must prove that there are laboratories under the ground in South Africa where gnomes are busy making diamonds. In both cases it is the principle of economy that automatically guides us to the more sceptical of the alternative conclusions.

Since first writing this, I have given a talk on the subject (Leeds, Spring 1987) and someone pointed out to me that the above account is rather over-simplified: all too often, he observed, people tend to opt for absurdly elaborate explanations of simple phenomena. In a desperate bid to defend my thesis I proposed that I had described the ideal situation when there is no intense emotional involvement in the subject. What he was pointing out was the way that Occam's Razor could be overthrown by strong feelings. In the above example: a scientist who felt very threatened by the possibility of paranormal forces might suggest a wildly elaborate conspiracy, that the television company and Uri Geller were both part of a world communist plot to overthrow the credibility of Western science; or the viewer who felt extreme spiritual claus-trophobia in the face of materialistic explanations, might conclude that the scientists were CIA agents sent to debunk Geller because he was a threat to the establishment world-view. Although I was wrong to overlook this other factor, it is surely still true that the overall reductionist tendency of the recent past has owed a lot to Occam's Razor as described here?

To return to the story: the Minister had obviously in the past explained his idea of a godless, causal world to the Pope, but he knew that it was only when the Pope had actually experienced such a world that he would really believe it; and Occam's Razor would then make it hard for the Pope still to believe in a god-full, transcendental world.

In fact (within fiction) what happened was that the Razor proved two-edged, and the Pope eventually abandoned the godless world as the bigger phantasy (though his vision of God had admittedly been modified in the process). In this way the story is a microcosm of this whole book, for I believe that many people would make the same mistake as the Minister.

In magical terminology, the phantasy principle and the sceptical principle are two gods, whereas pure logic is just a technique or tool. But because people do not recognise this fact they fall into the error of monotheism: for example they become totally identified with scepticism, lumping together 'scepticism', 'reality', 'logic', 'sanity', and 'common-sense' into a *summum bonum* which is the only real thing and yet is mysteriously opposed by a demon which lumps together 'unreality', 'phantasy', 'madness', and 'gullibility'. As a result of such identification they utter daft statements like 'it is illogical to believe in ghosts' - as if a cubist art critic were to protest that it was 'unruly' to sketch freehand curves, the ruler being simply a tool that has no relevance to freehand work, just as logic is a mental tool that has no direct concern with existence or belief.

Because the story is a microcosm of the book, it also explains its own purpose. In it I am trying to do the same as the Minister, trying to lead the reader to experience a fiction world in order to alter their view of the real world. If I had the resources of Macroc I could do this properly, but I haven't. Instead of running the program on Macroc I had to run it as best I could in the reader's own mind. If I had been able to employ a better programmer - for example the world's best short story writer - the result might have been more convincing. But let us look at some of the things that were programmed into the story.

First it had to be clearly fiction. Just as the Minister was constrained by the principle of uncertainty and could not reproduce the real world in facsimile, I could not hope to pretend that this story was true; to do so would have required much extra detail to make it convincing, and every detail would increase the risk of the story being betrayed by factual error. So I made it a clearly phantasy world, by adding such bizarre differences as a Pope who lived in a caravan.

On the other hand it could not be too bizarre, because I wanted the reader to accept it and live in it. The phantasy world needed, for the sake of realism, to have some surprises for us (like a Pope in a caravan), but it also had to have the decency to justify some of those surprises in a way that made us feel reasonably at home in the world. Therefore I filled in more detail in the main elements than was strictly necessary: more insight was given into the characters' motivation than is normal in a science fiction story, and more explanation of the Macroc model's mechanism was given than would be normally required of a non-science fiction story.

Having thus tried to win basic acceptance of the story's main elements, all further description was cut to a bare minimum. This was because I wanted the story to be modelled in the reader's mind and, knowing my limitations, realised that as long as a character was basically acceptable, the natural tendency for most readers is to create their own mental images to flesh out the action; while any inadequate descriptions might interfere with that natural tendency and cause the reader to reject the program. Just give the bare bones and let the reader imagine the detail.

As well as making the story as infectious as possible, it also needed to be purposeful. The very first sentence sets the theme: the Council Room is simultaneously silent and brilliantly sunlit. To a blind man it would be utterly restful in its silence, to a deaf man it would be utterly stimulating in its brilliance. This theme of one reality offering two contrasting interpretations crops up all over the place: the Pope's apparent idleness is described as a hero's struggle, the King's apparently childlike behaviour has a hint of Machiavellian manipulation in it, and so on. The idea is to make that theme - of one world with two contrasting interpretations - so acceptable that it becomes easier to apply it to our own reality at the end of the story, and therefore after the story has ended.

The message of this book is not an attempt to justify or prove artificial intelligence, it is more concerned with our own psychological reaction to that subject. My problem in discussing that is that many people are too caught up in the 'is it real?' game to be able to play with the possibilities. I want to say 'let us imagine our society beginning to believe in artificial intelligence on a big scale: how might that effect our entire world view?'. So the story took us on an imaginative trip into that situation, and it left us at the end with a hint of what I believe the effect might be. For I believe it could completely overturn our present ideas of reality and illusion, and restore rather than destroy the magic and mystery of existence.

The progress toward acceptance of a totally causal world where human genius becomes a programmable, mechanistic phenomenon, is a process of demystification or reductionism which shrinks our universe, making it smaller and smaller as our ideas of 'spirit', 'gods' and 'other worlds' are whittled away. But at the end of this process do we find a crystal of utter certainty as the Minister for Technology assumed? Or do we find a Black Hole where reality implodes into a rebirth of mystery, as the Pope seemed to discover? The next chapter will argue for the latter possibility; for that is the danger of the monotheistic error - we fall victim of the opposites.

The purpose of this present chapter was explained in the paragraph in the story where the Minister allows the Pope to run back over Macroc's software, to verify that even such apparently miraculous events as the creation of life really were no more than the effects of random processes. Having done my best to make the story as effective as possible, it was necessary to hack it to bits by analysis in order to reveal the mechanism and reinforce the point suggested in a previous chapter: that we already know how to model universes, we do so within our own brains.

5
Johnstone's Paradox

THIS CHAPTER IS CENTRAL to this book because it spells out most directly the paradox that I perceive in the completely materialistic model of the universe. It seems that the materialist, reductionist approach, if pursued to its logical conclusion, will not lead to the end of all mystery so much as a rebirth of that sense of wonder - a greater world with room for magic and mystery, we shall see. Earlier chapters prepared us to meet this paradox, later chapters will examine the consequences of it.

The 'completely materialistic model' I am dealing with is not a rigorous academic concept, but rather just a popular world-view. It is not so much what any one person believes in, but rather an approximation to the average world-view at the back of someone's mind when they say 'I don't believe in all that spiritual nonsense'. Because it is a vague, popular notion it has all the more power to tyrannise us, so I must begin by trying to pin it down, as follows.

The completely materialistic model of the universe assumes the following absolute facts.

1. The universe is finite.

2. All phenomena in the universe are subject to, and can be explained in terms of, a finite set of knowable laws which operate entirely within the universe.

The second fact is the most obvious one: it relates to the idea that there are 'laws of physics' which can explain everything. I call them 'knowable' laws, because any law that was somehow 'unknowable' would suggest transcendence and be too godlike to be acceptable to the complete materialist. I also avoid using the words 'determined by those laws' because the complete materialist can nowadays accept laws (as in particle physics) which have a probabilistic rather than a deterministic outcome. This was not the case in Victorian days.

But does the materialistic world have to be finite? Here I am on less certain ground. I do not know of any current materialist world view which assumes an infinite universe, but that might just reflect my ignorance. The Uncertainty Principle seems to be generally accepted nowadays, and gut feeling tells me that this principle would be redundant in an infinite universe: because an infinite universe can be mapped isomorphically into a subset of itself, and could therefore 'know itself' in a way excluded by the Principle. (Do other people's guts go in for that sort of feeling?) So the existence of the Principle suggests that the universe 'needs' the Principle and must therefore be finite.

What are the characteristics of a finite universe? Firstly it must be limited to a finite number of components. It would certainly be a severe blow to current materialist assumptions if it was proved that the fundamental particles were infinite in number, or were subject to an infinite number of independent inter-reactions. Secondly it must be limited in extent. This used to mean defining an 'edge' to the universe, outside which sat God, but now we tend to see it in terms of an unbounded yet finite model, as in the idea of a 'curved universe'. Thirdly, it should not be infinitely divisible. An example of this lies in the behaviour of electrons in an atom: they lie on discrete orbits and seemingly jump from one to other without giving any meaning to what we, in our imagination, can call 'the intervening space'. Does the materialistic universe have to be 'grainy' like this, or could it be 'smooth'? I'm not sure if the distinction is important to the materialist idea, except that smoothness is meaningless unless you have infinitely fine measuring instruments to detect it, and that is impossible unless you have either infinitely small fundamental particles, or some transcendental thing or omnipresent 'spirit' which can flow between the fundamental particles and so give meaning to the spaces between.

These three types of finiteness tend to be related when you think about it. In the above example we see that it is almost meaningless to talk about a materialistic universe that is infinitely smooth, and yet has only a finite set of fundamental particles - because we need an infinite set of infinitely small particles to make smoothness meaningful. Again it would be impossible to allow an infinite number of elementary particles in a finite universe which is not infinitely divisible: there would not be room for all those particles. Again, if we assume a grainy universe made up of a finite set of particles, then the number of permutations of those particles would also be finite; so, if we then insist on an infinitely extended universe, it would have to be a universe that repeated itself endlessly. In such a universe there would be scattered throughout space endless other planets identical to ours, with identical people behaving identically. But, according to the materialist assumption, such identical people would have identical consciousness, so in what sense could such a universe be meaningfully called infinite? Any finite observer would see only endless repetitions of a finite universe.

I don't want to extend this justification of my statements any further, because it is tangential to the point of the book. This book is not about absolute truth, but about our everyday perception of the world. When a typical materialist says that 'telepathy is bunk', he is not expressing a conclusion based on a lofty philosophical argument, so much as expressing a gut feeling that the universe is ultimately knowable (and therefore finite) and that we already know enough to have practically excluded telepathy as a possibility.

So I stick to my initial statements that a completely materialistic universe would be subject to these absolute facts:

1. The universe would be finite.

2. All phenomena in the universe would be subject to, and could be explained in terms of, a finite set of knowable laws which operate entirely within the universe.

Such a universe would be programmable, and so reproducible. Again it must be made clear that I am not assuming identical reproduction or total determinism at the atomic level. If a daffodil plant is a totally material thing, without any spiritual or etheric influence in it, then it is theoretically possible to describe every atom in every cell of the plant, to describe every reaction between every atom, and therefore to build a computer model of the daffodil which is complete and perfect in every detail. Even though, at the subatomic level, the computer model would have to allow for non-deterministic behaviour of particles (and it would do so by allowing the known probabilistic weighting to each likely outcome of an interaction), at the macrocosmic level such statistical irregularities are negligible and the result would be a complete 'living' representation of the daffodil as seen by a materialist.

Similarly, but on a bigger scale, it would be theoretically feasible to describe the entire neural network of the human body and brain, and all the possible reactions between its parts. When that was modelled into a computer the result would be the re-creation of the human mind and consciousness, provided we accept the materialist's belief that no outside agency or 'spirit' activates or informs our human consciousness, in other words that it is 'no more than' an effect of those reactions.

Finally, we could go the whole way, as in my story, and recreate the approximate initial conditions of the universe, and thereby reproduce a whole universe. A totally materialistic world would be a reproducible world. Putting it terms of the machine intelligence algorithm of Chapter 2, a totally materialistic universe would be precisely describable, and therefore programmable. Even if we face the limitation that certain elements of its structure could only be defined by a 'precise' probability function, we still get a universe that can reproduce itself. As was explained in the story: this reproduction of the universe is not a duplication, but is more like animal reproduction: the new universe would perhaps be as different from, and as similar to, the old one as a son is to his father. The subatomic uncertainty of the reproduction process would be expected to give the new universe different 'fingerprints' from its parents.

The argument can now be developed in two ways. The original formulation, as 'Johnstone's Paradox', is stronger, but harder to defend. So let us take the easy way first, because it is more in the spirit of this book. The original 'strong' version will be briefly dealt with at the end of this chapter.

We begin by assuming that we are in a universe that persists in fitting the materialistic model. In other words no irrefutable evidence of spirit, God, or the like is going to emerge in the foreseeable future. We also recall my observation that humans like to justify themselves by logic, but that there are also gut feelings that over-ride (or enhance?) logic. One such is the principle of economy I called Occam's Razor.

So let us imagine the steady advance of computer power through the stages I have outlined above. Having developed computing to the point where the processes of a single living cell could be modelled, the next step is perhaps the simpler one of clustering the cells and modelling their interactions, until the stage is reached whereby a complete daffodil plant could be modelled.

As this technique becomes widely available it becomes useful. For example a plant breeder could calculate a DNA code to produce an amazing new daffodil, the sensation of the Chelsea Flower Show: he could model various cross-breeds of existing daffodils, study the resulting models, and see which gets closest to the ideal daffodil he wants to create. Each attempt would grow in the software and be output as a full colour rotatable visual image on a high resolution screen. If the result looked interesting, then the breeder would go ahead and create it.

This process would take a lot of the uncertainty out of daffodil breeding! But it would also affect peoples' feelings about daffodils. This program would produce daffodils that were utterly mechanistic, the result of chemical interactions in their component cells. And they would look exactly the same as the real daffodils.

But some of us do not see daffodils in terms of mechanistic chemical phenomena. Some of us see daffodils as golden heralds of Spring, as a miraculous fanfares that defy dread Winter's icy grip to bring cheer to maiden's hearts and to turn young men's fancies lightly to thoughts of love. Although it is theoretically easy to hold both views simultaneously, in practice we tend not to. The same reductionist principle that makes it hard to believe in Uri Geller once we have seen a debunking conjuror perform the same tricks, will make it hard to view daffodils as well-intentioned miracles once their mechanistic principles have been fully experienced in a computer model.

True, we can still gaze in wonder at a good sunset, even though our knowledge of the atmosphere means we no longer see the ruddy hues as the flames of God's blazing chariot. But most busy city dwellers do not even notice the sunset. When we do, perhaps on holiday, enjoy a sunset we tend to do it as a deliberate aesthetic exercise, and almost congratulate ourselves for finding time to do so.

Explicable daffodils, like explicable sunsets, will lose their glamour: already some 'advanced' souls see no harm in sticking plastic daffodils in their window boxes, while primitives like me still shudder at the thought of such 'lifeless' blooms. Just as the Moon that men have walked upon can never again be so mysterious, so will the synthesising of daffodils tend to reduce their psychic value for most of us.

Now let us assume that, while we have been discussing daffodils, computer science has progressed further. The stage is now reached when the human mind can be modelled in a computer. It is at last possible to chat all day to a computer without realising that it is not a real living person. And how do we react to that? Occam's Razor will make it hard to believe that there are two quite different sorts of mind - the 'real human' and the 'mere machine' - which nevertheless have identical characteristics. As in the case of daffodils, we will most naturally tend to economise on entities, and decide that all minds are 'mere machines'. People will begin to fully accept that they are mechanistic phenomena - a view that receives quite a lot of lip-service already, but still mostly from people whose behaviour does not suggest that they really accept the idea in their hearts.

The evolution I am describing is unlikely to proceed in big jumps and at precise moments. Some people already claim to see themselves as machines, though very few appear to 'realise' that idea: most materialists are still making an intellectual stand whilst their general attitudes continue to betray a considerable unconscious acceptance of traditional ideas about the superiority of humanity - an attitude which I attributed to the Minister of Technology in my story. No doubt some people's ideas will run ahead of computer science: they will fully accept the idea of computer consciousness even before robots start to outperform humans at Wimbledon. Other people may lag behind, needing to see thousands of daffodils being faithfully predicted on their computer screens, before they can fully accept that daffodils are mechanistic.

Individual differences will be countless, but what is certain is that every step taken towards reproducing human consciousness in machines will further encourage public opinion towards seeing ourselves as machines; and the basic reason this will happen is because Occam's Razor will continue to erode the idea of man's 'spirit' by making it seem a redundant hypothesis. First daffodils become machines, then animals become machines, then men become themselves machines, and then...?

The end point of this growth in computer power is the ability to model an entire universe. Even if we never in fact reach that end point, as we get closer towards that possibility general public opinion will begin to accept the idea that a mechanistic universe could be created in a computer, just as a mechanistic human consciousness and a mechanistic daffodil had been created. And once again, Occam's Razor will make it hard to believe that our own universe could be anything but itself mechanistic.

But now we come to the paradoxical bit. Here we are living in a mechanistic universe, and there is the very real possibility that we will soon be able to create an utterly similar universe by programming a computer - ie by ordering the logic of this universe. But will Occam's Razor then still allow us to believe that there are two distinct types of universe - the 'real' and the 'computer' universe - which are nevertheless utterly indistinguishable to their respective inhabitants? Surely not! The natural reaction will be to accept that our own apparently material universe is not what we have long assumed, instead it is itself an 'illusion' caused by ordering the logic of some higher universe.

Once the idea of creating universes becomes acceptable, then there comes the idea of universes within universes within universes... It then becomes very hard to believe that we are somehow privileged to be inhabitants of the one original 'real' world - just as it is hard for people who do not accept divine privilege to believe that our Earth can be the only planet in the vastness of space which contains life.

The paradox is this: the reductionist process described relentlessly erodes and diminishes our world, but the end point of this process actually creates a bigger mystery than all the mysteries the process had previously destroyed: it suggests that our universe is an illusion that was created within another universe, an unknown universe.

So that is the 'easy' formulation of the paradox I have called 'Johnstone's Paradox', namely that:

Even if Artificial Intelligence never reaches the point of reproducing our entire reality, the more likely that possibility seems to become the more humanity will be moved to abandon the idea of a 'real' material universe.

This is the message of hope for those who detest artificial intelligence, seeing it only as a battle cry for the reductionists.

The original version of Johnstone's Paradox has been written up elsewhere[9], so will not be pursued at length here. It is harder to defend, partly because it attempts to deal with absolute realities rather than the commonly accepted realities dealt with in this book. So I will compress it into numbered paragraphs.

1. A mechanistic reality would be a reproducible reality.

This is argued as above.

2. A reproducible reality would reproduce.

This is the hardest bit to justify. It has only been justified in rather 'human' terms: there are many good reasons why a reality would need to reproduce, some of those reasons will be suggested in Chapter 7, they include 'overpopulation', 'over-sophistication', 'curiosity', 'claustrophobia' and so on.

3. Unless we make the difficult assumption that time has a finite beginning, then we should accept that this process of reproduction has happened many times, resulting in a mass of multiple and nested universes.

4. The existence of multiple universes means that it is statistically most unlikely that we happen to be living in the original mechanistic reality.

5. The reproduction of universes would not imply that all universes would be created the same, on the contrary, there would be endless variations from the original reality.

This bit was also hard to defend. It was partly defended on the basis of a universe's own 'unknowability' or uncertainty. But more significant changes were argued: it was suggested that if there was a universe where, for example, reincarnation did not occur, then it would be natural for its inhabitants to wish to create a new universe where reincarnation did occur, in order to see how well it worked! Again, these themes will be expanded in Chapter 7.

6. Hence Johnstone's Paradox: *If reality is ultimately mechanistic, then it is highly unlikely that this universe of ours is a mechanistic universe*

I thought that Johnstone's Paradox was frightfully neat. The problem was, it never caught on. The reason was that it tackled the wrong problem, for it was not whether God exists or not that matters, it is whether people believe that God exists. So in this book the arguments do not dwell long on The Truth, instead they concentrate on predicting the ways in which popular thought will adapt to advances in computer science.

Prediction is less aggressive than persuasion, more liable to promote laughter than opposition.

Johnstone made flesh.

6
Exploring the Paradox

THE PROCESS OF totally changing one's conception of reality is not easy: it is arguable that this cannot really happen within a lifetime. So the last chapter is hardly likely to have shattered your world-view, but I do hope it has at least suggested that the computer model of our universe is an idea which merits consideration; that it is at least a possibility rather than a total absurdity.

The following chapters will approach the subject from a different angle. They will assume the possibility of a computer universe, and will explore some of the characteristics that such a universe might possess. What we find is that such exploration has an intriguing ability to cast light on the nature of our own universe, indirectly supporting the idea that our own universe might be a 'computer' model, or rather a phenomenon created by an ordering of logic in some 'meta-universe'.

First I must explain how I intend to explore the model. Let us begin by exploring the idea of exploring an idea.

Take any novel idea: for example the von Däniken idea that this world has in the past been visited by advanced beings from outer space. Some people's reaction is to start collecting facts, searching history and exploring ancient monuments for evidence to support or negate this idea. Other people are more inclined to sit back and philosophise, toying mentally with the concept that we are not alone, that others might have visited us, wondering how and why they visited, what they did and why so little trace remains. Other people react imaginatively, putting themselves in the position of being spacemen landing on a primitive world, and imagining how they would react, and how others would react to them. Other people would explore the idea vividly, accepting it as true and seeing how well it worked as a vision of the truth. (These four approaches correspond respectively to the Scientific, Religious, Artistic and Magical mentalities as I described them elsewhere[10].)

Three of these approaches will initially be attempted in the coming chapters: the academic, the philosophical, and the imaginative ones. The vivid approach will be dealt with later as a suggestion for further research.

The academic approach means that there will be comparisons made with accepted or traditional ideas; of course, if I was being truly 'academic' there would be precise reference and actual quotation: instead there will be vague reference to commonly accepted ideas - because this is not basically an academic book.

The philosophical approach will allow us to ponder the idea of universes within universes and ask astonishing questions as to whether there has to be an original foundation, or whether the chain of universes might be infinite, or finite but unbounded like the snake which swallows its tail.

The imaginative method will mean inventing science fiction scenarios about possible ways people like ourselves might go about creating universes.

Then we will find that these different approaches tend to run together and throw light on each other. For example, the philosophical approach might ask whether a universe has to be willfully created by an intelligent being, or whether the logic of a universe might simply work out all its permutations and eventually hit on a new creation as a chance event (or an inevitable event, if it is the nature of such a universe to run through *all* its possibilities). This might suggest a science fiction story based on a chance creation of a universe by the ordering of chance events in our own universe: a dream which unexpectedly creates itself within a computer, for example. As we develop this story, we might find it surprising us by fitting certain accepted facts, or commonly held assumptions, and so being 'confirmed' by the academic approach.

Thus all these approaches will tend to merge, but it is helpful to have delineated them initially, because it will help to reduce misunderstanding. Some people are so good at approaching things in a particular way, that they give no validity to other approaches. If one reader is naturally academic, he might be very irritated by my science fiction flights if I had not first made it clear that they were deliberate exercises in phantasy. And anyone who is reading this book for a bit of science fiction escapism or for philosophical adventure, should understand why I make so much reference to more commonly accepted beliefs.

The intention is not to labour our exploration by being rigid about categories, but rather to indicate a choice of approaches to the core of this book's thesis.

To complete this chapter, let us give a sample exploration to illustrate the four approaches separately and in combination.

I begin with a philosophical exploration: the idea of simple elements having potential for creating complexity.

An undifferentiated space is a sort of zero in its own terms. It is tempting to argue that it is not a zero but rather a unity, for it is surely 'one space'; but we can in fact only recognise that oneness by stepping 'outside', or mentally separating ourselves from that nothingness, and looking back at it. As soon as the first difference, split or mark is made within that nothingness it has defined a unit. However, the existence of that one mark creates a duality: the marked and the unmarked. But this implies a trinity: the marked, the unmarked, and the implied duality between them. But this implies a quaternity: the marked the unmarked, their duality, and the trinity which includes them. And so on: the apparently harmless act of making a distinction is like cutting a slit in nothingness through which the infinity of integers tumbles into existence.

But to return to the beginning: I said that the one cut creates a duality, made of the marked and the unmarked. That is not really conceivable, because the unmarked is still nothing and so does not 'count'. It is only conceivable by considering the before and after state of the mark itself - ie the 'unmarked' is really just a label for an inconceivable state which we assume to have existed 'before the mark'. In other words this unstoppable flood of creation is born from the womb of Time. Just add one spare (unoccupied) dimension to a space, and you have created a potential for order, or sequence - the cut and the uncut versions of our universe can co-exist at different points in the extra dimension of Time. And order allows complexity through permutation or logical sequencing.

This philosophical exploration has gone far enough to interact with academic exploration. My observation about the fundamental nature of Time is found to be in keeping with the traditional astrological symbol of Saturn as the Lord of Time, and as the Lord of Restriction and Order, ie as a last defence before the trans-saturnine planets. It also reflects the traditional kabbalistic relation of Saturn to Binah the Dark Mother or ocean beyond the Abyss. So we find that there are well established traditions which seem to be in harmony with the purely speculative ideas of my philosophical exploration: in that sense the academic approach seems to support my speculation - not, I hasten to add, by 'proving' it, but simply by echoing it in a way that encourages further exploration.

Having made a bridge to the academic approach, let's look for other examples. There is a materialist theory of the universe (quoted in my previous story) which says that matter generated by chance during the Big Bang would tend to coalesce into galaxies which would include planets like ours, planets where chance interactions of atoms would evolve life - which would itself evolve intelligence and imagination as we know it today. This theory is not one I have invented, it is an idea that was common in scientific circles quite recently, and there are certainly books which expound it - therefore it is suitable ground for the academic exploratory approach. What is interesting is the light it casts on the original philosophical approach; by providing a rather more tangible illustration of the way in which the simple elements of a space (the elementary particles in three dimensional space), when supplemented by a spare fourth dimension (time), will tend to run through their permutations, and that those permutations will include combinations (molecules) which tend to order themselves into more complex structures, which themselves develop intelligence and an ability to perceive themselves.

What is intriguing is the development of imagination in this materialist model. It is intriguing because it is obvious from our own experience that the materialist universe can 'imagine' magic and gods. In other words it can not only perceive itself, it can also conceive things that lie outside itself - universes which must be greater than itself, because the original materialist universe does not contain magic or gods. The whole is greater than the sum of its parts, a quart in a pint pot thanks to Time allowing order.

To return to the philosophical approach, we see a claustrophobic tendency in such creation: order the logic of any universe and it will tend to create concepts too big for the universe they were born in. Overcrowding will be the motivation for creating new universes.

Our philosophical exploration is now sufficiently tainted with human feeling or anthropomorphism, that it now forms a bridge to the imaginative approach.

Let us therefore imagine such an overworked reality, an overcrowded universe. I wrote a short story on these lines for an earlier book[11], but will spare readers the repetition of it here, and limit myself to a summary. It pictured the limits of overpopulation of the globe as was discussed by some of our own scientists in the late sixties: a time when the entire surface had become one multi-storey city where people lived cramped lives fuelled by re-cycled synthetic foods. Those scientists argued that such a world would eventually cease growing when it became unable to dissipate the heat it generated. We further imagine that political power in this world is so sensitively balanced that no politician has ever dared to make a stand on population control; as a result of this procrastination they have reached crisis point. What can they do? There is not even enough spare energy resource left for a significantly large scale colonisation of other planets.

An obvious question is to ask how people tolerated this world in the first place. It was largely because humans have a wonderful ability to adapt to and take for granted whatever conditions they are born into; each generation had merely seen cramped conditions grow a little more cramped. However, there was also a service called 'recreational cybernetics' whose task was to keep people happy. They ran a sort of super interactive video service which did rather more than offer a choice of programs as our tv service does, for their machines could analyse each individual's character and current psychological state, and shape an entertainment program which was tailored to the individual's need. What is more, this program would be input directly into the individual's nervous system, so that it would be lived out like a dream, rather than watched upon a screen.

It was the recreational cyberneticians who proposed a solution. They said that their computers now had the power to model a whole new world, in fact a whole series of parallel worlds, and that they could read peoples' characters so completely that they could now reproduce their consciousness within these new worlds. As a result everyone now alive could transfer consciousness into a new universe, and dispense with their physical body in this world. All that need be left in this world is a central computer system running forever off solar energy, sustaining its own inner worlds.

The response to this suggestion was that all the experts got very excited, making plans as to what the new universes should be like; but no two of them could agree. So the chief cybernetician said that, given the timescale, there was not much that could be done but to scan and consolidate the peoples' racial memories in order to create worlds that were copies of our own world at the time when civilisation was just about to emerge. In other words, if we cannot agree on an ideal, let us at least create believable worlds of the greatest possible potential.

So this was done; and prominent people entered the new reality and came back to report that it felt just as real as physical existence - in fact even more real because the new worlds were so rich and exciting and vivid to people used to living in a sunless warren. Encouraged by these stories, the entire population began to forsake their bodies and enter the new reality.

The last person to go over was the chief cybernetician who had dreamed up this scheme. He found himself regaining consciousness in the body of a tribal sage. He looked up at the stars, and realised that he had made them. He looked at the strata of the rocks, and realised he had laid them down. He also realised that already children were being born into this world, children for whom the 'real' world would be no more than a myth. He had a strong desire to keep that myth alive, to preserve something for posterity. But he also felt helpless, because he had no pen, no paper, no word processor or printer. He realised that all he could do was to take the great stones and shape them...

So that was an imaginative exploration of the idea which began as a philosophical speculation. What is interesting is that it has thrown up a whole lot more material for the academic approach, because it has suggested a new theory to parallel, and rival, the von Däniken theory. What it suggests is that the myths of other worlds, of a golden age, of ancient wise ones etc could be based not on superior beings from outer space, but rather on superior beings who created this world and first populated it. Signs of precocious knowledge or advanced intelligence that appear teasingly in ancient monuments, might be mementos left by those who were taught by the original inhabitants of this world, rather than memories of visitors from outer space.

This theory lends itself to academic exploration because it could encompass all those little puzzling fragments referred to by von Däniken, but it avoids the two biggest snags of his theory. One is the absence of definite proof of space travellers: why have we not found any remains of flying saucers, if they had technology and materials superior to ours? The other is the elusive nature of subsequent visits: why aren't the spacemen trading openly with us now? The theory I mentioned is unhampered by these problems: people of superior intelligence and knowledge who were reborn as scattered individuals into primitive conditions would not be able to recreate their technology; all they could do would be to teach and erect monuments as a sign to later generations. The rest of their life would be a matter of survival.

As well as providing material for further academic exploration, this idea re-fertilises the initial philosophical exploration by raising the possibility of multiple parallel universes. Did the rest of the population end up on other planets in this universe (and is space travel leading to a cosmic reunion?) or were they reborn on identical worlds in what people like to call 'another dimension'?

This example has shown the various approaches to exploring the idea of a computer universe, how they can be pursued separately, and how they also weave together and sustain each other. What I have not yet illustrated is the 'vivid' approach. This is less easy to illustrate as it is a matter of experience; any description of it could make it sound like a mixture of the other approaches, because it does not convey the experiential factor.

Consider the von Däniken enthusiast who travels the world to explore his ideas. You find him in the South American wilderness, getting excited about the precise placing of archæological remains. Such people come in two main types: there are those who look up from the rubble and exclaim 'this is yet another of that preposterous fool von Däniken's obfuscations. This stone is far too small to be a sighting stone, and its position in the alignment is obviously the work of nineteenth century restoration'; and there are those who will be heard saying 'look at all this incredible evidence, how can the establishment go on denying it?'.

It takes a lot of enthusiasm to go to all these far-flung places just to poke among the rubble, the chances are that people who do so are involved in the vivid approach, that they are allowing themselves to 'believe' or 'live out' a myth or theory. The first type is living the myth that he is a crusader against this charlatan von Däniken who has made a fortune out of bogus scholarship and hare-brained ideas, while honest academics cannot raise the cash for proper research on the subject. The second person is living the myth that there are advanced intelligences 'out there' who have tried to communicate with us and may be trying again. As they stand in these remote ruins, away from the confusion of everyday life, the little signs described by von Däniken grow in importance and help them to 'tune in' to this idea of flying saucers. They feel that, as 'aware' people, they might even invoke the return of these advanced visitors, and a miraculous solution to the ills of the world. By allowing the idea to become real, they become more sensitive to scraps of evidence that would be dismissed by the first person as false or at least 'inconclusive', and so feed the academic approach. In their desire to picture the sort of beings that left these signs, they stimulate the imaginative exploration of the idea. The vivid approach also interacts with the other three approaches and thus weaves into the whole.

This is the problem as I see it: we are encouraged by our education to become specialists, and that makes us suspicious of broad, un-specialist arguments like the one in this book. As said earlier: many people are disturbed if they come across a bit of sci-fi fantasy in the middle of what looks like a pragmatic argument. The feeling is that the one could corrupt, or somehow cast doubt on, the other. But I believe that this sense of 'creeping rot' in fact stems from the lack of clear boundaries in the disturbed person's own mind. If the distinction between approaches is first acknowledged, as I have done here, and the possibility for constructive interaction is also explained, then it will be easier for the reader to dance with me through the coming chapters. At any point you can decide for yourself which approach I am using, and judge for yourself how good are the links I suggest.

So, in subsequent chapters we will explore the idea of a universe based on ordered logic and its relationship to various areas of human experience. We will be using the academic, the imaginative and the philosophical approaches, and the mixture of all three. But I won't make a point of differentiating the approaches; the purpose of this chapter is to give the reader the tools so he or she can make their own distinction as and when needed.

To repeat: some people are weak on some approaches and can get upset when they sense that they are being used. This reaction can be so strong that it obscures the value of the actual idea being explored. But my purpose is not so much to present a convincing argument, as to give examples and encourage the reader to explore the idea themselves, and so to prepare for the vivid approach - which is ultimately the most exciting in my belief.

7
Johnstone's Paradox and Creativity

THE CONSIDERATION THAT the universe we perceive might be created from the ordered information of a meta-universe opens up a host of wonderful possibilities for this universe, possibilities that the rest of this book will explore. But it is a curious quirk of human nature which makes one promptly turn one's back on the potential treasures of *this* universe, and begin to wonder about the meta-universe. What is it like, and why did it spawn our world?

The exploratory nature of this book is constantly being re-emphasised, for I am very wary of the reader who could suddenly lose interest because it looks as though I am trying to present an argument based on unjustified assumptions. One of the most dangerous areas for unjustified assumptions is the meta-universe. If I argue (as I will later) that this universe is likely to allow free will, because free will makes for a more interesting world, then I am assuming that the meta-universe is interested in interest. It would, therefore, be wrong for me to deduce that free will *must* exist; instead I must limit myself to 'it is likely to exist' or even 'it is a myth in which I need to believe'.

Because there are dangers in making assumptions about the meta-universe (even that it exists), but in recognition of the fact that it is utterly natural to make such assumptions, this chapter will jump right into considerations of the meta-universe and the reasons for its creating our world. By tackling this straight away, we may keep later chapters a bit cleaner.

If the Johnstone's Paradox argument was presented as a logical argument, it would founder on its assumption that universes which could reproduce would reproduce. Starting from the materialist view of a finite world made of a finite number of elements constrained by a finite set of laws: although such a universe could be modelled, why need it model itself? Perhaps the task is too big or complex?

Consider an analogous problem: if we accept that life could originate as a result of a chance ordering of molecules, does that mean that life *would* originate? If there was an ocean containing all the right stuff in all the right conditions, would life develop, or might all those trillions of molecules just bumble through eternity without ever hitting on the right combination? Seen in these terms, I think that if life did not originate eventually then I would want to know a reason why not. Similarly, even if we deny any intelligence or purpose (or even illusion of purpose) to the meta-universe, and see it as no more than a chaos of interactions, then I would want to know why those interactions never at any point fell into an order that created a universe. Why should the meta-universe end before it had done everything? I am suspicious of the suggestion that it might become locked in closed loops of interactions (and therefore not run through all permutations), because closed loops are just the sort of ordered structures of logic that I would expect to lead eventually to the creation of a universe.

The above paragraph proves nothing, but it does justify my temperamental inclination to believe that universes would reproduce if they could. I made a big effort to start from the minimal assumptions about the psychology of the meta-universe, describing it as a mindless mass of random events. Let us now repeat the conclusion in more sensible language.

It is natural for a universe to want to try everything, and that includes creating another universe.

I am not quick to dismiss the materialist model, because it has scored some notable successes. According to the materialist model this world of spiritless matter has, by chance interactions, created the human mind. Within the human mind are all of mankind's dreams. Those dreams include many visions of universes peopled by gods, angels, devas and other spirits which exist in parallel with the world of the senses - most primitive societies have lived their lives entirely within those dream worlds. Therefore we see that a materialist world is able to create worlds that transcend itself, contain more than the original universe.

As the structures that evolve within the materialist universe grow more and more complex, they can conceive ever more amazing extensions of their world - witness the most far-flung imaginings of the science fiction writers. So even a purely materialist universe can evolve claustrophobia, grow too big for itself, become overpopulated with entities. Out of the dry-as-dust mechanistic universe of the nineteenth century rose the heady creativity of Wagner; if ever there was an example of mechanism seeking to transcend itself, that was it. And that is another reason why I am temperamentally inclined to accept that a world which could reproduce would reproduce.

A science fiction writer can create his universe, but it might remain a totally unshared experience, lifeless in the eyes of the world. On the other hand the Nazis created a parallel universe - one similar to ours except that it was manipulated by an international Jewish conspiracy - in which millions of people lived for a while, and some people still do live in it. But even that world was not universally acceptable: we still have a long way to go to the world described in my short story, a created universe of which even the most convinced opponent would be forced to admit the validity.

The Jewish conspiracy universe was not complete enough. To take an easy example: a philanthropic Rothschild, who reads that his financial empire is an attempt to corrupt civilisation, will find that he cannot get into the Nazi universe, because it is too small to accommodate certain elements of his experience - eg his own philanthropic intentions.

So, if we are to build a universe big enough to contain mankind, it will need to be very finely wrought, neatly finished, devoid of awkward loose ends and inconsistencies. Having illustrated my acceptance of a basic creative or 'art' urge in a universe, I must now illustrate examples of a corresponding perfective or 'craft' urge.

Such signs abound. For example: in the pre-publicity for a recent television series which detailed the early history of the Christian era, a lot of emphasis was placed on the careful research and authentic treatment of the subject - right down to an attempt to dress the actors in robes made of materials constructed according to the techniques of that era.

What am I getting at? There is an argument current which opposes artificial intelligence, saying that we do not *need* machines which think like humans, therefore will not develop them. This argument runs counter to human nature which has shown a traditional fascination with artificial creation of homunculi, one that bears little relation to need. Necessity might be the mother of Invention, but Non-Necessity is the sexy trollop next door that really sets Invention's pulses racing. I expect to see an enormous investment in human endeavour, all directed at an attempt to model our world in its entirety.

But it will not stop there. Creating a universe is the ultimate art-form; one could almost believe that all art is but a rehearsal for this final human triumph. Although there could be very specific purposes for a new universe - as in the Minister for Technology's solution to the religious question, or the resolution of the population crisis described in the last chapter - so much more would be done out of sheer curiosity. As said above, intelligence soon outgrows its environment and claustrophobia sets in. If we finally prove that there is no spirit, no magic, no god, no free will, no reincarnation, no fairies, no... then it will be artistically necessary to create worlds with all these properties, just to see how they turn out - 'if God did not exist, it would be necessary to create him'. Once that is done, we are brought back to Johnstone's Paradox: a totally materialistic universe would tend to spawn multiple non-materialistic universes, therefore it is statistically unlikely that we happen to be living in a totally materialistic universe.

Another consideration is 'free will'. People tend to identify the idea of a 'computer universe' with determinism. Certainly the idea of total mechanical determinism can sit very comfortably in the vision of a world that is based on the ordered information of a meta-world. But I do not favour it myself, because I think free will is more fun, and the reader will now realise that I am temperamentally inclined to favour fun as a big motive in universe creation.

Firstly I am not keen on the idea of a totally determined universe, where God knows exactly what the outcome will be, (and just sits back yawning and waiting for it to happen?). As was suggested in my short story, even if a universe runs to a determined program, it is such a complex program that its outcome could only be predicted by running the program itself. So a totally pre-determined universe would suggest that God is re-running the program for a second time, or for eternity. Boring.

The only sensible version of predetermination which I can conceive in passing is that God had wandered into a universe that was coming to an end, that he did not like the conclusion, that he sought to improve on it, and that he created a program which would run backward from the poor conclusion to determine the initial conditions which created the universe; and that he is planning to create a new universe which improves on the old one by altering the initial conditions slightly. In this version we happen to be living in his backward-running program, and that explains how he already knows the outcome of all our actions. Less boring, but rather hard work.

No, I think God likes a bit of surprise (and if he doesn't, then he can't hope for much worship from this quarter). So he put in a bit of free will.

I don't intend to divert into lengthy attempts to pin down what is for me just an act of faith tangential to the course of this book. But some people can get stuck on the very concept of free will within ordered logic, so let's enlarge slightly on the possibilities.

Firstly I would argue that we don't need much free will. As I have written elsewhere[12], consider a simple example: a feeling of hunger. I might respond by eating a chocolate biscuit. Or else I might think ahead and not eat the biscuit because it might spoil my appetite for a nice lunch. Or else I might eat that biscuit because, although about to go to lunch, I want to take the edge off my appetite in order to spend less at the restaurant. Or I might make myself eat both, because the doctor advised me to eat more carbohydrates. Or I might eat nothing that day, as a gesture toward third world starvation.

These examples show how my consciousness can operate at many different levels. Now it is possible that we are machines and that, at any of these levels, our apparent decision for or against the biscuit is in fact an illusion, as it is totally determined by past conditioning of our brain cells. But that does not exclude the other degree of freedom: we still might be able to choose which level we are 'deciding' on. Just a little freedom is needed in a world which is largely predetermined.

A remark made by the Pope towards the end of the story is interesting in this context: he described the flow of time as being 'turbulent' and therefore unpredictable. If you consider the difference between smooth and turbulent flow in, say, a stream it can cast light on this. When the flow is smooth, you can make adjustments to the flow upstream and predict what will happen downstream: if the strength of flow is ten percent too strong for a boat's moorings you can reduce the flow at a weir upstream by more than ten percent and be sure you have saved the situation. This is not necessarily so in the turbulent case: reducing the flow upstream might actually alter the eddy pattern and rip the boat right off its moorings. During a severe hurricane you will notice that the damage occurs in a crazy, haphazard fashion: the tree on the hilltop is unscathed while the big oak in the valley is felled by an eddying gust.

A turbulent flow has a mind of its own, because it is a 'logic machine' made of innumerable fluidic 'flip-flops' and logical gateways which interact. Whereas the smooth flow needs big changes to produce big results - eg a ten percent decrease in flow at the weir to reduce the strain on the moorings by ten percent - the turbulent flow can act with all the alarm of a conscious entity - a tiny pebble dropped into flow upstream could just cause the ripples which will alter the eddies so that a river cruiser downstream is torn from its moorings. That is why the Pope had to be so careful about his interactions with the sub-universe, dropping a pebble that saved Moses' life was an act which altered the world in a way that he could not predict. So he could not justify such action in the logical way the technologists demanded, but only in terms of his sense of 'God's Will' - happily, the common people could understand that.

In a turbulent flow, and time in our universe seems to be a turbulent flow, the minutest changes can have immense consequences - the justification for the belief in magic, perhaps? This sort of rationed free will would fit my observation pretty well: for all our individual pride, most people's lives do in fact run largely to predictable formulae of birth-marriage-death and its standard variations, with turbulence between these rocks making it impossible to predict their precise timing or expense, so I favour those philosophies like Gurdjieff's which see spiritual development as a growth away from an innate, mechanical nature. The fact that there is strong evidence for determinism being a large part of our universe (as in scientific theory) and of our actions (as in psychological theory) does not upset me in the least. These laws are welcome as the warp and weft of the canvas upon which we create our personal embellishment in times of illumination. We can always look *back* on events and see the mechanistic explanation of them, but the turbulence of time makes it impossible to mechanistically predict forward - except by running the program that is life itself, running in real-time!

Anyway, free will gives this universe value. In the final analysis I can work out, independent of dogma, the most logical action to take. Then I can take that action, or I can use a random number generator to decide an alternative action. Then I can choose between the logical and the random action, and I can choose absurdly for my own secret purposes. By not telling you what those are, I will stop you getting into my mind to argue that my decision was mechanically determined anyway. Just let's get on with this chapter!

Another interesting possibility emerges from considering this world to be a work of art. Our artists have long been interested in the relationship between their art and its public; in other words 'interactive art'.

A painter is often interested in the idea that the picture painted is going to be hung in a situation of the buyer's own choosing. A composer knows that the performance of his music could be affected by feedback from the audience. Some art sets out to cultivate and incorporate this interaction between art and public. This element is very important in an art-form that is in its infancy but which, I have elsewhere predicted[13], will become highly developed; namely the interactive computer game. I anticipate the day when the game in the video arcade will respond not just to the button-pressing of the player, but also to more subtle responses like the alteration of skin resistance in the hand on the joy-stick (as in present day lie detectors), the relative split-second hesitation or assurance of the player's reactions to surprise images on the screen or words spoken. Such a game could analyse the player as he plays, and adapt its tactics to the personality, creating a 'game' that would be a profound lesson in life, or initiatory journey, for the player. There is nothing intrinsically fantastic about such a development and, unless Japanese industry grows tired of making money, I am sure such games will appear when the required computer power becomes cheap enough. But it does illustrate another possibility for our universe: might it be an interactive 'game'?

Although some artists might create universes as spectator sport, universes which could be 'read' like novels or watched like films, there would be other artists who would want to involve the spectator in their creation. They would want to create a link that would allow the spectator to live out the new reality more fully, by entering into it, and even by becoming involved within it.

There are problems about such involvement, as was suggested in the short story about the Pope. In another version of the story (not included here), the characters were a High Priest and a Magician/Technologist. The Magician was less open than his counterpart in our story, he did not spell out his intentions to the High Priest before luring him into the inner world. When the High Priest got an inkling of what was happening, he bolted back to the outer world and removed the Magician's helmet from his head so he could not get back to the real world (thus casting Lucifer out of heaven). So the subsequent action revolved around an illusionary world created by the pride of Lucifer (the Magician/Technologist), into which God (the High Priest) had imprisoned him; and the two wrestled out their problems within that world. Then came the time when God wanted to incarnate: Lucifer said it would be an absurd thing to do, because it would mean subjecting oneself fully to the experience of time (whereas their existence as 'spirits' in the world passed like a dream, millions of years that did not clash with their sense of real time). But this only made God all the more determined to become man and so redeem the world etc etc.

Given that there are such problems in an interactive universe, what could we do about them? The crudest approach would be the 'spaceman' approach: simply to appear in the universe. The reason this is artistically unsatisfying is that it corrupts the original artistic creation. Imagine a superb soap-universe, a sort of heart-rending cosmic Coronation Street containing all human passions; it has millions of fans watching it avidly, then the system goes interactive and an eager fan suddenly appears within the universe, apologises for his incongruous clothing and explains that he has come from 'outer space' or 'another dimension'. Bang goes the plot: the characters would forget all about their romances in the excitement of this discovery. So the 'spaceman' interaction would have limited artistic value.

The next obvious approach would be to let the consciousness of the viewer become more or less thoroughly clothed in the mind and body of an inhabitant of the universe - as with the Pope in the body of the young cow-herd. Once again, a total invasion that knocks out the original mind would blow the plot, because the character would act totally out of character and create a counter sensation. More realistically we would need to 'graft' the mind into the existing mind, as the Pope did. The problem here is, how far do we go?

The natural escapist tendency would be to want to drop in totally, to retain all that is possible of the character and only insert the spark of ego awareness that would allow one to experience the other world. The viewer is so thrilled by the handsome hero that he wants to plunge right into his being, without in any way diluting or molding the character. If this is done totally successfully, there is no longer any interaction: we are once more just spectators, but from a different viewpoint. But as soon as we step up the interaction there is a problem of survival in what might prove to be a stronger mind than your own. If the hero was admired for his tough, forthright manner, then the sense of transcendence instilled by another human will joining forces with his own natural will, could transform the hero into a tyrant. The interactor becomes trapped in the passions of a vicious bully.

Interestingly, one of the myths of Atlantis suggests that this did in fact happen: that the first attempts of the angels to enter into the animal bodies of the hominids, and so create mankind, resulted in a race possessing the knowledge of the angels but the passions of the beasts. The higher minds of the incarnated angels were swamped by the lower minds of the bodies they had entered, and so the Atlanteans grew corrupt and destroyed themselves with their precocious technology. 'Are we repeating the mistake?' is the question this theory poses.

I see problems in interacting with a universe, whether by jumping in as a spaceman, or taking over a body. Elsewhere[14] I suggested a further approach, analogous to the relationship between a horse and its rider. Imagine an interactive universe, and imagine that we can enter it as 'spirits' associated with a body, rather than at one with it. Compare this to being a rider of a horse, rather than entering the horse's mind. If we entered the horse's mind we might be swamped by it, for example we might be competing in a race with a mare, when equine sexual passion could overthrow the human will and turn the race into an orgy; so there is safety in being detached, as a rider. That safety is paid for dearly: it demands a long period of 'breaking in' and training the horse to respond to the rider's control. Only the most experienced rider reaches that point where horse and rider become one: a whole greater than the sum of its parts.

The pleasure of this model of interaction is that it is strongly suggestive of the traditional relationship between a human and the 'higher self', 'guardian angel', or 'daemon': an entity that is part of us, yet not part of us. This is a juicy idea that I will save for the 'religion' chapter as this one is getting too long.

In fact, I've almost forgotten what the point of this chapter was, so let's recap.

I began by being a little anxious about the natural tendency to assume that the universe which created ours is one which would be inhabited by people like us with similar motives. Sometimes the best defence against a natural tendency is not to attempt to resist it, but rather to indulge it to exhaustion; so that's what I did, thinking that the reader could then have the fun of reading later chapters to see if my method has worked.

So I began by presenting reasons why *we* would try to create universes, and what sort of embellishments we would want our universes to have. To compensate this indulgence I tried to consider an extremely different case: the universe which has no purpose, no will, no creativity, no mind - what would it do? Here it was less easy to find examples, until I realised that there is a strong body of opinion which asserts that *this* universe contains no purpose, no will, no creativity, no mind, for this universe is just a mechanistic working out of the random possibilities inherent in the conditions of the Big Bang. Bingo! I can therefore claim that such a random accretion of molecules would deliberately create a universe with free will, because it would value the interest of such a universe. Of course I know my words 'deliberately', 'value' and 'interest' cannot be taken literally; instead they must be interpreted as representing those meaningless pseudo-concepts which we imagine that we perceive in our world. So for 'deliberately' read 'deliberately', for 'value' read 'value', and for 'interest' read 'interest', if you wish to avoid confusion.

I feel that my rambling exploration looks like an argument that pulls itself up by its own bootstraps. You're not supposed to be able to do that. But how could a universe be created out of nothing, except as an argument pulled up by its own bootstraps? There is an example of that in the next chapter!

8
Johnstone's Paradox and Religion

CONSIDERING JOHNSTONE'S PARADOX in the light of humanity's religious traditions, one uncovers some fascinating paths to explore.

For a start there is the religious idea that this world is an illusion. In some religions, such as Buddhism, this is stated most explicitly; in others less so. Even in Christianity, the religion of the western materialist, we find some ambiguity: on the one hand the Church is keen to show by its social commitment that it is not a 'pie in the sky' escapist institution; on the other hand there is also a strong undercurrent of ideas about the vanity of this impermanent world. So the Church will actively fight against poverty, despite a faith which sees poverty as a noble qualification for entry into the kingdom of heaven. The idea here is not to be cynical about the Church's social involvement, but rather not to let us forget that there is another side to the story when I speak of the Christian belief in the illusory nature of this world.

All together this adds up to the remarkable fact that the large majority of the population of this world pay at least lip-service to the idea that this world is an illusion. Even particle physicists hold a qualified version of that view. This is a rather remarkable, and quite hard to square with the 'common-sense' man who thumps the table with his fist and says "This is what I mean by reality!".

This split, between the vividness of matter in everyday life and the religious belief in its falsity, could be at the root of many problems, for it can be resolved in three harmful ways. First it is possible to be so involved with one's belief in the worthlessness of illusory existence, that one becomes absurdly unworldly, a hopeless misfit and failure in the material world. This then provides ammunition for the second group: those who reject religion because the material world is so vivid that it makes religion seem like fantasy - a pity, because religion can be a lot of fun. The third group are those who manage to live both lives, but in watertight compartments. These are those who call themselves religious and who attend church with genuine devotion, but who live the rest of their lives just like materialists. Such people strongly denounce, for example, the commercial spirit of Christmas, but feel very threatened by, for example, the hippy family who really do live in peaceful poverty. None of these groups manages the difficult task of bridging the gap between the need to live our lives and the sense of illusion that seems to haunt us.

If this book is correct in predicting that we are going to evolve a new view of the universe, then the change should do much to resolve this split in our nature. We do, in times of worry or lonely meditation, sense that life is somehow unreal, yet we have no graspable notion of how the unreal could also feel so real. We are surrounded by traditional notions that 'life is but a dream', and that there lies an invisible reality beyond this world, but we have no way to square such ideas with our current materialistic world view. 'Other dimensions' will remain just a convenient cliche until we have started to create those dimensions ourselves in computer memory.

What I predict is that this gulf will be bridged as we approach the creation of universes by ordered information. Even if we never finally get there, as long as the public begins to live with the belief that ordered logic might be able to create a new reality, that a computer might see itself as a real person, then the public will begin to get a real experience of how this world could be an illusion whilst being utterly vivid to our senses.

As is the style of this book, I can again present arguments to support this new vision. Once again I must point out that these arguments are not in themselves sufficient for most people, but simply that they illustrate the sort of arguments which will act like flux to help the solder of shifting feeling to stick in the public mind. Most people do not alter their world view on the basis of clever arguments, but on a combination of shifting public opinion plus personal experience.

Why should mankind so widely embrace the idea that the world is an illusion? It is hard to explain the persistence of this belief on utilitarian grounds, because the idea itself can be quite a block to material progress. In fact any attempt to explain this belief in totally materialist terms sounds tortuous beside the simple alternative explanation: that men believe the world is an illusion because it really is an illusion.

This realisation could have come to us in many ways. Perhaps our world was originally populated by refugees from the higher world - as in the overpopulation story discussed in Chapter 6. In which case the idea could be a universal folk memory of the refugees' original teachings, distorted and diversified by millennia of oral transmission. Perhaps the occasional visitor enters our world as an avatar, as in the story of the Minister for Technology and the Pope. In which case we again have garbled accounts of their teachings as passed down by people who did not yet have the understanding of what a meta-universe could be. Or perhaps the techniques of mysticism are in fact techniques for raising one's consciousness into the 'lower' level software of this universe and so experiencing a vision of its machinery. In that case what we have is the distorted accounts of mystics who grappled to convey to us what they had experienced in regions which lay outside our human language.

In all these cases you find an explanation which is most intriguingly fruitful. Study traditional ideas in the light of these possibilities, and wonderful correlations will be found. For example the curious idea that 'in the beginning was the word', and other traditions where the world was created by naming its parts: doesn't this tally well with a teacher from a higher world trying to explain how ordered logic or 'words' of digitised information are the basis for creating the illusion of this world?

For descriptions of contacts with the 'higher' world we have to study the writings of the mystics, but there is another, more accessible, body of experience which could be equally or even more relevant. Most people can develop a relationship with their dream world, so that they can consciously communicate with the characters within it. Some people can do this much more vividly than others: Jung, for example, whose experiences of communicating with inner 'spirits' are recounted in the book *Memories, Dreams and Reflections*[15]. Indeed Jungian literature is full of stories of those who have been able to visualise dream characters and talk with them. These examples show that such dream characters behave independently of our own wishes, and are autonomous in their personality. They therefore form an independent universe within our unconscious minds. According to popular theory this unconscious universe is not so much a 'spirit world' as a product of our own brains, something totally dependent on its functioning. This means that this inner universe is an example of the sort of sub-universe that this book is discussing: an 'illusion' formed by the ordered logic of our brain structure.

What is interesting is the relationship between a person and his inner universe. Has anyone asked their dream characters if they believe in our universe out here? Do they realise that they are in an inner universe? I do not know the answer, but there is evidence to suggest that such dream characters see themselves as gods who have created our universe, who are more real than our 'real life'. They seem to believe that they are independent of the individual's brain.

Jung gives an example of the 'spirit' Wotan which he detected in many German minds before the Second World War[16]. He warned that this spirit saw itself as an ancient and universal god of old Germany, and that it would be prepared to drive Germans to massive self sacrifice to serve its own ends. Indeed his prophecies were largely realised: as when Hitler under Wotan's supposed influence attempted to order the Luftwaffe to bomb the remains of Germany, rather than face the humiliation of defeat. Clearly Wotan saw himself as a universal god that had mankind as his pawns, rather than seeing himself as a dweller within a universe created by the workings of the human brain.

This suggests that the relationship between our world and a meta- universe could be far from clear cut. Even if the meta-universe idea seems to fit all observed facts, there will be many who will prefer to see it as a useful hypothesis, or workable fiction created by ourselves, rather than the real foundation of our existence. Indeed the problem of inner and outer, of whether or not the meta-universe and God came first or whether we invented them, of whether the laws of physics 'actually exist' and so on may never be resolved one way or another. Perhaps truth lies midway? Where the hell is midway?

Considering such examples will show how useful the new world-view could be as reconciler between religion and common sense. Yet it is the religious person who is perhaps most inclined to resist this reconciliation, and deny the basic idea. The reason is that the religious person is likely to have pre-conceived notions as to the nature of the creator of this world. Such a person is very likely to be upset by my examples such as the story of the Pope and High Priest; so much so that they will believe that I am trying to present them as truth, rather than illustrations to help smooth the way to comprehension.

I would have a certain amount of sympathy with someone who read as far as Chapter 4 then exclaimed that he had no time for an author who believed that the world was created by a nasty Minister for Technology with dubious motives. Such an idea does violence to our ideas of Divine Purpose. Even in less extreme or personal terms, there could be something offensive in the idea of a 'computer' universe with its suggestion of prior calculation, a suggestion that might not tally with some notions of this world being a spontaneous outpouring of divine love, or whatever.

If the reader reacts violently against this idea, then refer back to the description of the battle against reductionism in Chapter 2. The inspiration for this book was my own horror at the computer universe. Over the years I have come to see that I have been battling against the sceptic within myself; my tendency to be angry about the 'sneering rationalist' was my own problem which has found its solution in Johnstone's Paradox. Because I could sense many other people who shared this problem of a battle between faith and scepticism, therefore this book was justified. So if any reader feels overpoweringly - and without, of course, justification - that I am trying to replace a loving creator with a 'clever-clever' boffin, then please think again.

First it should not be forgotten that some heretics quite close to home have themselves suggested that it was not God who created this material universe, but rather Lucifer. This version was reflected in the alternative version of the Pope story that I discussed in Chapter 7, where Lucifer made the universe in order to deceive God.

However, apart from such considerations, we can also speculate that perhaps the meta-universe prior to ours is not an absolute, but rather just one step in a chain of evolution which was initiated by a truly transcendent deity.

Rudolf Steiner is a mystic who has described his spiritual vision of the creation of this universe in his book *Occult Science*[17]. He saw three prior universes before this one, making four levels of creation - the Saturn, Sun, Moon and Earth stages he called them. Only the last one (our one) is made of matter. The Moon stage is rarified, like a dream world, and the Sun and Saturn stages even less concrete. At each stage a universe was born, went through its entire evolutionary cycle to reach its ultimate expression, before being 'reborn' at the next stage - a process very reminiscent of my description of a universe that needs to reproduce when it has exhausted its own potential.

Steiner's account of what he saw by his own mystical vision is by no means unique or eccentric: there are other traditions of nested universes which range from the more primitive myths of animal gods who spewed out other gods who finally gave birth to our world, to the cosmic beaurocracies of certain gnostics. But Steiner's creation is so similar to the Jewish kabalists' account that I will now concentrate on this version of the story.

The kabalists define ten stages or 'sephirah' in the creation of a universe. The first nine stages lay the foundation, as it were, (the ninth is actually named the 'Foundation') and then comes a 'fall' into manifestation which is the tenth stage, the universe itself. This jump to the tenth stage is described as a definite leap, crisis, or change of state, it is not just a smooth transition that rounds off a gradual development. As such it is strongly suggestive of the point when, all the software having been completed, the program is run and the new universe is 'suddenly' a new reality. The 'fall' to the tenth sephiroth has that same quality of a total change of state into a new order of reality.

What is more, they too describe three entire generations of existence, or universes, before this material one. Each is less solid than the one that follows it, so I will describe them backwards. This world of matter is called 'Assiah', a word which includes not just the actual matter, but the energies, etc that it involves. This world was created as a consequence of the completed evolution of a prior universe called 'Yetzirah'. Yetzirah is not a world of matter, but of something much more tenuous that is described as the World of Images. We might compare it to a 'dream world'. The inhabitants of Yetzirah are called 'angels'. It in turn was created as a consequence of the completed evolution of a prior universe called 'Briah'.

Briah is not a world of images, but something much more tenuous. We might call it the World of Ideas, understanding that ideas are abstractions which lie behind any attempt we make to cloak them in imagery: the word 'seat' is an abstract notion which does not properly have an associated mental image until we qualify it further as in 'Arthur's seat' or 'my driver's seat'. Briah is inhabited by personalised ideas called 'archangels'. Briah was in turn created as a consequence of the completed evolution of a prior universe called 'Atziluth'.

Atziluth is not even a world of ideas, but of something yet more tenuous behind ideas. As we have now retraced evolution beyond a point where language could be conceived, words become difficult; but we can approximate to the idea by calling Atziluth a world of 'possibilities'. It is 'peopled' by gods. The attempts of the theory to wrestle with the description of how this indescribable universe was itself spawned by God from the Unmanifest will not be described here. Be warned: they are a little like my own painful efforts to conceive a universe growing from a 'cut' in nothingness (Chapter 6).

In this Jewish version of the story it is the world of angels which conceived our world, when their world had reached completion. What does 'completion' mean? The various possibilities already suggested - overpopulation, claustrophobia, boredom-inspired curiosity etc - could all have played their part, but whatever the angels' apparent motives the Jewish model sees the divine purpose of God lying behind it all. So this is an example to show that it is possible to describe the creation of our universe in quite humble terms - eg 'the angels needed something to do' - without necessarily denying or restricting the omniscience and omnipotence of the god that lies behind the whole business.

This Jewish story also raises a philosophical question about Johnstone's Paradox. The basic version of the paradox makes the minimal assumption that universes just keep spawning universes endlessly - 'minimal' in the sense that once you accept that a thing *can* happen the next obvious assumption is that it *will* keep happening unless some other extra factor (like 'God' or 'the end of time') steps in to constrain it. So the obvious first assumption is that we will create another universe which will itself eventually create another, and so on. Applying this to what I have so far said about the Jewish version, we would expect that this world would eventually create another even more solid world

- just as our material world is more solid than the angels' world (it is hard to imagine a more solid world - perhaps we would cut out all that quantum uncertainty rubbish in the next attempt - but then it was perhaps difficult for the angels to imagine what our world would be like). But the Jewish tradition I'm quoting has a different story, for it claims that these four worlds were all that was intended in the divine plan, and that this material world is the lowest point of evolution after which we involve back up through the other worlds towards God.

This would suggest a different long term future to the one I seemed to be suggesting in Chapter 5. Actually this is not so. Remember that the point of the Paradox that I am making in this book is not one of absolute truth: I am not saying we *will* make a new universe and that *proves* the universe is an illusion. What I am saying is that we will begin to believe in the possibility of creating universes, and this will totally transform our view of the world we live in. In these terms there is no clash with the Jewish model, for the acceptance of Johnstone's Paradox could mark the turning point between evolution and involution. It could mark the point when mankind for the first time develops a clear understanding of the machinery of our universe and is able to turn attention back toward the world of angels, without becoming obsessed by the crazy notions that have haunted us in the past. Johnstone's Paradox could be the voice of God calling us home.

There is another aspect of the religious question that I would like to touch on in this chapter, and that is the question of morality, life's purpose and the problem of evil (won't take long to sort out that little lot...). Once again I am obliged to create a 'story' in order to encourage your imaginative involvement in what I am saying; and once again it will be couched in our own human terms. But once again I hope the reader is able to understand these limitations and not be bogged down in the human detail. What matters is the principle the following example is trying to convey, not its exact formulation.

Imagine a sort of 'brave new world' where technology has played its part in eliminating poverty, disease, famine and war. As a result the population had increased, not to the nightmare state of the 'overpopulated' world of Chapter 6, but to a stable equilibrium where there was no waste space left: plenty of excellent recreational parks with automated rescue services, but no real wilderness or unexplored arctic wastes remained. Having tamed Nature, the only problem left was man's own nature.

The problem was what to do with our basic instincts to struggle, to compete, to face danger and challenge, in a world which has eliminated all dangers. There were more or less crude technological solutions such as drugs or mass brain surgery, but such solutions were morally unacceptable to a people who had triumphed because of their own in-built aggression. Sport provided some outlet, but was so very much 'just a game'. Army-style 'assault courses' were devised, but they too had the feeling of being just games. There was no longer any wilderness where the young folk could go out with minimum equipment and prove themselves against Nature; so any solution had to be an artificial one.

What was done was to create a primitive, amoral universe 'red in tooth and claw'. In that universe were created hominid creatures with developed brains and suitable limbs for holding tools. Into this universe the people of the brave new world would be sent in order to build their character and 'discover themselves' through struggle.

How could they enter this world? It was necessary to become deeply involved, because any half hearted relationship with the world would reduce it to just one more elaborate 'game'. The first approach was to be born in full consciousness into the body of one of these hominids. That lead to disaster, because the brutal passions of this harsh world proved too strong for even the most enlightened wisdom of the minds that entered it. What happened was that the hominids developed sudden super-intelligence and a precocious technology, but were utterly at the mercy of their animal instincts. As a result they almost wiped themselves out by war. This was the story of Atlantis.

Fortunately there were survivors. The world was left to recover while a new approach was devised. When the world had settled down and Atlantis was just a memory of traditions born by a few of the more intelligent hominids, then it was entered again. This time they did not enter into the conscious minds of the hominids, but into the unconscious minds, with rather different effect. Instead of being at one with the ego of their hominid, and so directly at the mercy of its passions, they were now in a position analogous to a rider on a wild horse. Keeping that element of 'separateness' saved them from the possibility of total disaster, but it did nothing to reduce the excitement and danger in other respects. Indeed, there was even more challenge in trying to wrestle for control - or even communication - with the body one was living in; it was like having to break in a wild horse before you could even set out on your planned journey. This was the frontier where our young people went to learn the lessons of life.

Of course, what I am suggesting here is that the over-civilised world was the world of angels. A world that had its own initial challenges and lessons, but which began to outgrow its own potential - it became all too easy. Therefore our world was created as a 'university of life' to provide a testing ground or course for spiritual development, and thus to restrict the spread of evil.

To see how this works in practice, let's take an example. Imagine a young angel called Ram. Being rather full of himself he chose as a freshman to take first incarnation as one prince Rameses in ancient Egypt; but he would rather not say too much about that now, because it was a disaster. Power and wealth went right to the head of Rameses. As a result he was forced to accept a string of rather humble and difficult incarnations - a slave in Athens, a poor saxon after the Norman Conquest, a negro slave in America, a prostitute in Bristol's dockland - but he is very proud of the fact that the young negro slave had a moment of mystical experience before he was lynched. That meant that, as 'Higher Self', he had actually achieved direct communication with his incarnation's lower mind - not bad for a fourth life. Now in his tenth year of schooling, Ram has a much more realistic idea of his potential. Of all the incarnations he was eligible for, he chose the one due to be called John Ramsey. This impressed his tutor, for John was an unglamorous incarnation, an (probable) only child to a shaky marriage, but it was a case of a child with high genetic potential for intelligence being born into a backward environment: the sort of high-risk incarnation that might be chosen by an angel with a plan to get ahead. Ram is horrified by the scrapes he has to get John into, but eventually the teenage John begins to wake up to the fact that he is not using his potential. Then starts a slow but steady rags to riches success story. It isn't all progress: Ram forgot one of the lessons of his first incarnation, that success attracts the attention of the hooligan element - those young angels who have not yet got licence to incarnate. As a result success almost goes to John's head in the form of demonic possession by an unqualified spirit - John is caught up in the materialistic rat-race. Ram manages to avert this by catching John alone one evening, where he sees an old woman weeping and begins to think back to his family and his origins. Thus begins a new phase in John's life, a time when he grows to accept a sense of purpose in his existence, a sense of some higher nature trying to guide him. Although he never really comes to terms with it, it has its effect on Ram. When Ram comes out of that incarnation, everyone notices the difference. Some essence of John now lives on in Ram, and will survive through future incarnations as they grow together towards fulfillment.

Cutting out the schmaltz, we have here a very interesting model which weaves together the ideas of reincarnation, a higher self, a spirit world, and of karma. It was illustrated at greater length to illustrate the sort of way it can be developed, and it can fit both traditional religious views as well as one's own sense of an elusive spiritual purpose.

Just add a dash of Hallelujah - and you've got a whole new religion!

9

Johnstone's Paradox and Science

In this chapter Johnstone's Paradox is explored in the context of science. Just because this book is full of references to computers and to universes, does not mean it is 'all frightfully scientific' as my mother would say, bless her. In fact I consider it to be rather unscientific, because science has largely followed the Aristotelian method, as opposed to the Platonic.

I wanted to avoid using those terms, but they seemed convenient. The trouble with dropping big Greek words is that someone is sure to have just read the original writings and will attempt to banish this whole book by saying 'that's not what Plato said at all'. So let's not be too pernickety about it. Anyone who reads graffiti and jostles with the holiday crowds at Clacton will quickly discover that, in the eyes of Joe Public, Plato was the one who sought to explain this world in terms of some 'higher' world beyond the senses, while Aristotle distrusted such notions and sought truth within the world of the senses. If that is the popular meaning of those words, that is how I will use them. And if that is not the popular meaning, then sorry: I'll seek other adjectives for a later edition.

In practical terms science is all about defining laws that precisely explain, and can therefore predict, observable phenomena. But if I produced such a law, say Newton's Gravitational Law, it would not be very scientific unless I provided an Aristotelian explanation of its mechanism. It would be no good saying 'this law holds because God has ordered matter to love and cleave to itself', and just leave it at that, because that is an explanation that lies outside the material world. Even to provide a model that is based on curvature of the space-time continuum, like general relativity, is not very acceptable. Scientists will suffer sleepless nights until a recognisable 'graviton', gravity particle, or at least a gravity wave, has been discovered. No explanation that calls on a world beyond all reach of even our technologically extended senses, will satisfy traditional scientific opinion.

Johnstone's Paradox, on the other hand, is all about explaining this world in terms of some meta-universe beyond the senses. So it would appear to be utterly and irredeemably Platonic. But there is an important distinction that I want to make here.

The Platonist looks at this world of the senses, with its extraordinary mix of beauty and squalor, the sublime and the ridiculous, and says that to explain all this there 'must be a higher reality behind it all'. This is like a jump from the world of the senses, an act of faith. Making this assumption, he now finds evidence fitting it; but he knows that any direct vision of the higher world cannot come through his senses, but only through the development of 'higher senses', or mysticism. This gulf which cannot be crossed by the senses remains, even for the most advanced sage: it means that he can never reveal his vision to the senses of the uninitiated, to them it will always remain 'mystical' and unreal.

Johnstone's Paradox, on the other hand, suggests that the process of minutely describing this sensual world, and coding that description as digital signals, will lead us to create worlds beyond the senses. So the highly Aristotelian discipline of artificial intelligence will lead us to real experience of 'worlds which lie outside time and space'. Platonism has been hampered by its need to look outward towards the supersensible, but Johnstone's Paradox allows us, by invoking artificial intelligence, to look inward from a meta-universe.

At present, if someone speaks of a world beyond the senses, he speaks of something which most of us can only comprehend intellectually, if at all. We do not have any sense experience to make the idea 'vivid'. But a future generation which has had experience of computerised universes, and which has had experience of sitting up all night with a psychotic computer that thinks it is Napoleon, and which has heard computers crying because someone didn't like the feel of their keyboards... that generation will have had so much day-to-day experience of other worlds that the concept of them will have become vivid. It is as though they will have grown a sixth sense which can grope out of space and time. Plato's higher worlds will be immediately acceptable without that initial blind act of faith.

There is a definite distinction here which I find hard to put clearly: that is why I have illustrated this book with stories to catch the imagination. Perhaps another analogy would help: it would be difficult to write a book about the social impact of television for 18th century readers with no idea of radio waves that can travel 'instantly' round the world; such a book would be full of appeals to the imagination. It would be far easier to write it for an early 20th century readership because one could use radio as an analogy: the idea that information can travel through space would be more acceptable to people who had begun to experience similar phenomena. For a modern readership, however, the book would pose no problem and the writer could concentrate fully on its message. In the same way, a generation brought up on Johnstone's Paradox would be much happier with Platonic theory than us, for they would have less difficulty in accepting 'higher worlds'.

Rudolf Steiner predicted that the year 2000 would see the schism between Aristotelian and Platonic thought being bridged. He saw these two great streams of thought being at last united. This is how I believe it might happen: as a gradual shift in man's attitude to this world, a shift that brings the two approaches together, rather than by a revolution amongst scientists, converting them into mystics.

One of my concerns in the last chapter was that some people might reject my whole thesis because they thought that it reduced the status of God to a programmer. In this chapter one of my concerns is for those people who might reject my apparent materialist assumptions 'because science now accepts a mystical view of the universe'.

There is a strong tradition amongst occultists and spiritualists of trying to gain respectability in the eyes of science, as I have argued elsewhere[18]. In the nineteenth century, when magnetism was all the rage in scientific circles, a whole school of spiritual theory emerged couched in terms of 'subtle magnetic fields', 'animal magnetism', the 'magnetic trance' and so on. When the luminiferous ether was being suggested as a scientific hypothesis, then there appeared a wave of occult theories about 'etheric fields', 'etheric bodies' and so on. In this century the idea of the fourth dimension caught the occult imagination, and we had talk of 'higher dimensions' and all that.

The tendency is for occult and spiritual theorists to catch a scientific hypothesis that they can relate to - suitable hypotheses tend to be the newest, most talked about, and as yet least rigorously tested ones - and see in them a 'confirmation' of spiritual/occult principles.

As I have argued in my previous work, the resulting theories are mostly pretty valid as spiritual/occult theories, but they remain unacceptable to the scientist. Usually science moves on to new hypotheses, and leaves the occult jargon sounding pretty corny to scientific ears.

The latest such scientific bandwagon is the extraordinary behaviour of fundamental particles according to quantum theory. We see the seeds of a new school of occult theory being sown in such books as *The Tao of Physics* and *The Dancing Wu Li Masters.* Again I want to emphasise that I am not denouncing these excellent pioneering books and their fascinating revelations, I am merely very cautious about those who quote them to illustrate that 'scientists now accept a mystical view of the universe', or some such phrase.

What we are seeing is science crossing a new frontier, making discoveries which challenge present concepts. This is something that has happened often in the past, and it always marks a time when science and mysticism come close to each other. Scientists find themselves 'groping in the dark' and being forced to make guesses about the unknown, being forced to make the sort of 'act of faith' that I described the Platonist as initially making, simply because there is a temporary shortage of solid theory; while mystics find in the confusion of the scientists strong correlations with their views about the illusory nature of reality. This has happened often enough before, and it has usually lead to a new set of pseudo-scientific occult terminology being developed. What does not happen is a widespread acceptance of mysticism by scientists. Instead they press on to find new laws which make sense of the current confusion; and they will refine those laws until they are as rigid as they can make them!

In the very long term, I personally do see science moving closer to mysticism, but I see it happening in small steps, some forward and some back, perhaps better called a 'wave motion'. The fact that there are at present some very mystical speculations amongst scientists does not guarantee that science has finally embraced mysticism, and that this book is forty years too late.

Having ticked off those who jump at *The Tao of Physics* and quote it as proof that their occult theories are now respectable, I would like to demonstrate my fundamental human sympathy for such deluded idiots by doing the same myself. I will quote briefly and in summary from a long previous article of mine on the subject, where I referred particularly to *The Dancing Wu Li Masters* [19].

First two quotations from that book:

> "In 1964 J.S. Bell, a physicist at the European Organisation for Nuclear Research in Switzerland zeroed in on this strange connectedness in a manner that may make it the central focus of physics in the future... One of the implications of Bell's Theorem is that, at a deep and fundamental level, the 'separate parts' of the universe are connected in an intimate and immediate way."

> "In short the physical world, according to quantum mechanics is... not a structure built of independently existing unanalyzable entities, but rather a web of relationships between elements whose meanings arise wholly from their relationship to the whole."

Now that is very much how I would describe the elements of a universe which is based on the ordered information of a meta-universe. If a scientist within such a universe is studying a hydrogen atom within the same universe, then he is made up of a vastly complex 'program' which calls up millions of generations of sub-programs. Amongst those sub-programs will be those which govern the behaviour of the individual atoms of his body, and of the fundamental particles within those atoms. Now it would be ludicrously uneconomical if that hydrogen atom that he is studying was governed by a totally separate set of programs from the programs of the atoms within his body (this argument will be amplified in the next chapter), and so there would inevitably be some link between observer and object, as there would be between any two elements of the world. What is more, this link would be extremely intimate, even though extremely subtle: we are parts of one great whole.

There is quite a tradition of demands from scientists for a theory which links us all into a greater whole. It is as though the remnants of the excluded Platonic method resurface from time to time in an attempt to compensate the separatist tendency of the Aristotelian method. There was a Renaissance fascination for models of the 'structure of the universe'. There was the luminiferous ether which pervaded everywhere, there was the space-time continuum, morphic field theory which links all creatures of one species even when they are physically separated, and Bell's Theorem as quoted. The resistance to all such theories is not that scientists don't want a unified universe (quite the contrary), but they cannot accept the connection unless it is measurable and detectable to the senses. They want the connection to lie within the material world, not without. It might need the 'sixth sense' extension of Johnstone's Paradox described above, to break down that resistance.

According to *The Dancing Wu Li Masters*, it is beginning to seem that a 'particle' is not so much a solid object as a collection of possibilities. Even when not in collision, a particle could be constantly splitting and reforming in a dance of 'virtual particles', so called because they break and reform too rapidly for observation or measurement.

If the simplest units of matter are so very immaterial, what about the concepts of time and space? We talk of a particle being generated at point A, accelerating towards a point B where it reacts with another particle. Is it the same particle when at A and at B? Our intuition that it is the same particle is supported by several observations. Firstly the particle seems to obey the laws of motion between A and B, secondly we can cause it to pass across photographic emulsion where we find a definite trail recording the particle's passage. However these 'laws of motion' are a pre-existing assumption in our thinking, and that is dangerous in an area where observations seem to be affected by our deeper assumptions. Secondly a close examination of the photographic emulsion shows only a trail of dots where individual molecules of the sensitive material have been activated: billions of separate particle detectors rather than a continuous locus. Physicists are no longer so confident in claiming that from this we can be sure about the motion of the particle between each molecule: all we can say is that at some point in the time interval *a* particle was present at each of the molecules along that path.

Bearing this type of speculation in mind, I would like to present a dishonest analogy. Having done all I can to assure you that the 'computer universes' of Johnstone's Paradox do *not* imply universes running in ordinary computers that we would recognise as such, or even necessarily universes within a some bio-computer like the brain, but rather a much more general and abstract concept that ordered information on one level can create an illusion of reality at another level; having done everything to extend the concept beyond silicon chips, I am now going to ask you to envisage a very naive picture of a universe created by a super calculator. Instead of a device based on binary logic, imagine one which evolved as a dedicated decimal arithmetic calculator, but which evolved to such power and complexity that it was able to model an inner universe. We are now going to imagine what the particle physicists of that inner universe might find if they tried to uncover their own 'fundamental particles'. I will describe it in terms of their reality, but add capitalised notes to reword it in the terms that we in the meta-universe would use to describe what they are investigating.

The scientists [A SET OF 'HUMAN PROGRAMS'] are investigating phenomena [COMPLEX CALCULATIONS] in their reality, trying to find the fundamental particles. There is an ancient tradition that matter is composed of indivisible 'atoms'. In recent centuries they managed to isolate these atoms [NUMBERS] which seemed to be the building blocks from which all objects [COMPLEX CALCULATIONS] were formed. But the new science of particle physics revealed that these atoms are not indivisible, but have a definite internal structure. They consist of a nucleus [DECIMAL POINT] surrounded by a cloud of particles [DIGITS] which lie in definite orbits [DECIMAL PLACES]. For example the atom 365 consists of a 3-particle in the third [HUNDREDS] orbit, a 6-particle in the second [TENS] orbit and a 5-particle in the first [UNITS] orbit. The particle physicists further discover that they can add energy to the atom and make the 3-particle, for example, jump to higher orbits, making 3065, 30065 and so on. They have also matched the dreams of their early alchemists by transmuting 365 into different atoms - eg 305+60, 280+20+65 and so on.

Having discovered that atoms are not indivisible, they want to know what is indivisible. They go on to isolate ten elementary particles 0,1,2,3,4,5,6,7,8 and 9, nine of which possess antiparticles (-1,-2 etc), but then begin to find that even these particles are divisible (9=3+3+3, or 2+7 and so on). For a while it looked as though all could be resolved into just three fundamental particles, -1, 0 and 1, but then 1 was itself successfully split into a 3 and a -2. Since then high energy physics has successfully split it into a 7 and a -6, two -4s and a 9, and several other combinations. In fact current speculation suggests that every particle is a bundle of possibilities which includes every other one as 'virtual particles'.

This is the standpoint of their 'new physics', whose theorists are challenging the traditional assumption that these basic particles obey the laws of macroscopic matter. For example, the 3-particle that jumps from the third to the fourth orbit as described: is it a unique particle which actually crosses the space between the third and fourth orbits, or is the 'space between' a meaningless concept? In what sense is a 9-particle in one atom the same or different from the 9-particle in another atom: or are they just two manifestations of a '9-field' which permeates all of the universe? When a particle moves through space [IS ASCRIBED TO A LINEAR SEQUENCE OF POINTS IN FOUR DIMENSIONAL CO-ORDINATE] is it valid to argue that it is a discrete physical entity actually following a one-dimensional locus through space?

I will not pursue the analogy further, because it is obviously imperfect and is based upon a very unlikely and clumsy model. But I hope it has nevertheless suggested that the sort of things which would be observed if the inmates of an 'ordered information' universe decided to seek for fundamental particles, are indeed strongly suggestive of the experiences of modern physics. When such people began to examine the 'close grain' of their reality they would come up against the limitations of the meta-universe's programming, and the results would appear quite illogical in their own accepted terms. Referring to the kabalistic model of the last chapter: is this truly the bottom point of a descent into 'matter', or will we be able to continue the sequence and create an even more solid universe where atoms really are indivisible?

In this chapter I have explored the Paradox in the scientific context, trying to show how it is distinct from science, yet could prove very relevant to its future. I have avoided extending the exploration into such fringe sciences as parapsychology, because these will be examined more fairly in the next chapter.

10
Johnstone's Paradox and Magic

As I BEGIN THIS CHAPTER which considers Johnstone's Paradox in the context of magic, I feel obliged once more to explain that this is a very general book that is concerned with popularly understood concepts rather than precise distinctions. Under the umbrella heading of 'magic' I am therefore going to consider: astrology, divination, dowsing, reincarnation, spirits, parapsychology, and the tarot, as well as ceremonial magic.

In lumping all these into the 'magic' category, I am not in this book picking any arguments with those who, for example, consider astrology to be a science and would be upset to see it listed in such disreputable company. My earlier book *SSOTBME* was devoted to a consideration of the fine distinctions between such topics and science, and will not be repeated here in case it stops you rushing out to buy a copy.

In *SSOTBME*[20] I also analysed the theoretical differences which distinguish such topics from science and from religion etc (by 'theoretical' I mean the mental processes and assumptions of those who practice such arts). But, for the purposes of this chapter, I am concerned with only one basic distinction between these subjects and science: that is they all assume that our universe is rather more 'connected up' than scientific theory would allow.

The special importance of this chapter, which it shares with the 'Religion' chapter, is that it deals with a lot of elements of our universe which would superficially seem to be excluded by the advance of artificial intelligence. Referring back to that talk described in Chapter 2, the immediate reason we wanted to protest against the speaker's thesis was that he seemed to be presenting a vision of the world which excluded all possibility of magic in the present sense, and of religion. The Minister of Technology's solution to the 'religious problem' in the story could just as well have been a solution to the 'spiritualist' or the 'superstition' problem.

So what I would like to do in this chapter is not just to show that Johnstone's Paradox is in keeping with traditional magical ideas, but to show that it positively supports them. In previous chapters I was content to show that we could explore this theory in the context of art, religion and science, and that we could find it fitting many of the traditional concepts in a way that both illuminated them and supported the paradox itself. When it comes to magic on the other hand, I am dealing with subjects which are likely to be considered rubbish by the average reader. So it is no good looking for support for my thesis amongst ideas which are largely outlawed: instead I will try to unite these outlaws into a 'vagabonds union' under the flag of Johnstone's Paradox, hoping that unity will be strength. Thus, although the reader may have severe reservations about nine tenths of the subject of this chapter, we may yet as a combined force present a possibility worth considering.

Connectedness: that is the crux of the matter. In the last chapter I suggested that the main thrust of science in recent centuries has been Aristotelian: a close analytical approach to the world which divides it into its separate components in order to understand it - 'divide and rule'. In dividing reality, science has divided itself: splitting into a myriad separate disciplines requiring such specialised knowledge that it becomes hard to be expert in more than one area. There has been a shortage of the process which would balance this separating tendency, the 'bringing together' which the holistic philosophers are now asking for.

The alchemists' formula for progress was *solve et coagula*, recognising the equal importance of both of these processes: it is necessary to analyse to gain understanding, then it becomes necessary to bring together or re-synthesise in order to gain wisdom. If we consider twentieth century science in isolation then it is hopelessly unbalanced; but if we practice what we preach and see it as part of a greater unity or historical process, we could be delighted that it has done the 'analysis' bit so well, because it has set us up for a really super 'synthesis' to come.

Let's start with dowsing. Someone claims that he can detect underground water using a pendulum (or hazel wand) while walking over the surface of the earth. According to current popular scientific assumptions that is impossible, because there is no connection: nothing links the underground water to the diviner. We can however point out that, even in scientific terms, there are several links. There is a gravitational link between all matter in the universe: if a flea jumps on our Earth it has a gravitational influence on the planet Mars which could be calculated mathematically, even if it is too small ever to be detected. There is also a sound made by running water which would cause vibrations in the earth. There are also geological correlates with underground water which produce visible signs on the earth's surface... and so on. So there is no lack of connection, but still the average scientist would feel that none of this is sufficiently strong to justify dowsing as a consistently worthwhile way to prospect for water.

Many dowsers do not even need to be present at the physical location: they can detect hidden water on a map of the area even from miles away. To argue that the cartographer has created a connection with the area, and therefore a link to the water, would certainly not satisfy a scientist.

Astrology is another example which can be considered at two levels. It is possible to present a rather weak case that the gravitational influence of planets is not totally trivial, because it seems to be able to affect sunspot activity. Therefore, in view of the extremely delicate neural reactions within the brain, it is not inconceivable that planetary positions at birth might via cosmic rays leave a long-term imprint upon a person's character - hence the validity of the horoscope or 'birth chart'. But such arguments will do nothing to justify 'horary astrology' which is the branch of astrology which specialises in answering direct questions. If, for example, you lose your keys, then the horary astrologer would consider the planetary pattern at the moment you asked the question 'where are my keys?' and would provide an answer based on that consideration.

The scientist would wonder what the hell could be the connection between the position of the planets when the question was asked (not even at the moment when the keys were actually lost, you see) and the location of those keys. Those who accept horary astrology merely on the empirical basis that it works, cannot usually answer the scientist's objection.

There are hundreds of systems of divination - from tea-cup fortune telling to the I Ching. To attempt to find a theoretical justification for every one of these so diverse techniques is to invoke a whole host of the sort of weak theories I've mentioned above; unless, that is, we look for a unifying factor.

There are two unifying factors which suggest themselves. One is that the input from each system is processed by the mind of the diviner; so perhaps the positions of the planets, of the tea leaves, of the tarot cards... are really just random 'hooks' upon which the diviner's own intuitions can hang? So, for example, it would not really matter if the horary horoscope was totally miscalculated, because astrological interpretations are so vague and so complex that the diviner's own intuition could still see what it wanted to see in the outcome. This theory replaces all the separate 'magics' of the divinatory techniques with the one big 'magic' of unconscious intuitive powers. It does therefore do a good job of bringing together apparent chaos. However, if you have a lot of practical experience of divination, you are likely to find examples which, if explained by this theory, would make enormous demands upon our belief in the powers of intuition.

I therefore favour the second theory which says that the connection between the question and the planetary positions, the tea leaves, the order of the tarot cards etc is 'time'. They both happened at the same time. In this theory, even if the horary astrologer miscalculates the horoscope, the important thing was that even the error itself happened at the same moment that the question was on the astrologer's mind, and is therefore not irrelevant to the question; thus even the miscalculated horoscope still has a certain validity.

If it is assumed that every occurrence which happens at one moment in time is somehow connected, then any system of divination becomes a matter of reading signs which are really there. Which is not to say that those signs are necessarily at all obvious - we may again be relying quite heavily on intuition - but perhaps they are clearer when the field of observation has been deliberately chosen or even set up with that question in mind; in other words it is perhaps easier to divine by looking at a tarot spread than by looking at the way the crumbs happen to have fallen on your bread-board.

Astrology is here perhaps an exception because we do not 'set up' the planets; however, their positions are so utterly predetermined and beyond our control that the horoscope could be seen as a much more precise and complete encapsulation of a moment in time than the position of those crumbs on the breadboard.

Now it is impossible to fit that 'time' link into the materialist model of the universe, because it implies a instantaneous connection between events separated by a long distance. One could however dilute the idea slightly and say that the connection is not actually instantaneous but travels at nearly the speed of light, so we can scarcely tell the difference. But it would still be hard for the materialist to accept that such a mass of information could be conveyed so rapidly: how can the positions of the planets at 10:37 convey so much information about the astrologer's client's marriage prospects, and at 10:45 be equally informative about a second client's choice of career? Meanwhile other astrologers around the world are receiving equally informative answers to other questions, and other tarot readers are shuffling their cards, and other I Ching readers are counting their yarrow stalks...

In the materialist model this adds up to a picture of widespread human folly. Another interesting point is that this form of delusion seems to have sprung up independently at all quarters of the globe, among all races and creeds - suggesting once more a non-material information link. However, if we accept that the fundamental reality of this universe is not matter, but ordered information, then an instant information link between all parts becomes much more conceivable. It even seems highly likely.

When we zoom through the enemy troops in a computer arcade game, we are not amazed that all those separate little monsters all move at identical speed; we do not examine the screen closely in astonishment to see how they can keep such perfect formation while moving so fast. That is because we know that the 'world' on the screen is an illusion, and that those troops are not having to judge their relative positions by taking bearings from each other. Instead they all receive their control signals at the same time from the 'invisible world' of the computer software.

Similarly, within the software of our universe, there runs a set of very low-level programs which we, from our 'internal' viewpoint, only vaguely comprehend under the name of 'collective archetypes' or 'gods' (this will be amplified later). At any moment of what we call 'time' those gods are in a certain relationship which is intrinsic (is that the word?) to that moment of time. This information is input into all programs, and so informs all observed phenomena simultaneously: for example it shows in the positions of the planets. Now the latter is an interesting example, because it is, in our apparently chaotic world, one of the most regular and predictable of all phenomena. Therefore it is likely to be the most transparent 'window' into the way those basic gods interact and evolve their relationships. That is why mankind has tended to align his gods more or less closely with these heavenly phenomena - they form a so much more 'transparent' window into the gods than the crumbs on any breadboard.

For example: the relative orderliness, or the relative randomness, of the pattern formed by those crumbs at any moment, might be a source of information about the relationship between the cosmic forces of order and the forces of revolution at that instant, but it would demand a careful statistical study of such patterns before we could learn to tell the difference; on the other hand, the present relationship between those forces, being represented by Saturn and Uranus, is much more obvious in the horoscope of that moment in time.

The above illustrates the spectrum of possible reactions to the practice of divination.

First we can say it is all bunk; when asked why it is so widely practised, we can reply that humans are naturally gullible; and therefore risk the rejoinder that perhaps the belief that divination is bunk is itself another example of human gullibility.

Second we can examine each method in turn and try to find individual theories that could explain the individual systems; thus creating a mountain of weak speculation.

Thirdly we could unify the whole subject by saying that the actual techniques are largely irrelevant, and it rests entirely on the intuitive skills of the diviner; quite a good theory, but it has to bear a lot of weight, and it does not help us with the rest of this chapter.

Finally we can unify the whole universe and say that every phenomenon which marks a point in time will inevitably show signs peculiar to that moment in time; that leaves us with the problem of trying to recognise and interpret those signs. Of course, our own minds are themselves phenomena which mark each point in time, so the theory also covers the question of clairvoyance, which is a system of divination that does not depend on any observation of outward signs at the time of giving a 'reading'. In fact the theory even unites to the previous theory in the sense that it sees both the divinatory objects (planets, tea leaves...) and the diviner's intuition as products of the moment in time, and the process of divination is therefore a reaction between these two factors.

This last theory is so strong, however, that it raises its own problem: why are we not all perfectly clairvoyant? why do we need other systems of divination if the answers lie in our own minds? You could answer briefly by linking to the previous theory, saying that intuition is the clairvoyant faculty, and it needs props to help support it. But this is a more serious problem which will be returned to at the end of this chapter.

Before leaving the topic of divination, however, I would like to do something that I have mostly avoided in this book, namely to quote from another book. In von Franz's *On Divination and Synchronicity* [21] she says:

> "Richard Wilhelm describes the functioning of the I Ching quite typically by the following picture. The relationships and facts of the Book of Changes could be compared with the network of an electric circuit, which penetrates all things."

She goes on to say that this sort of concept is basic to the Chinese world view. Later in the chapter she is describing the unconscious as a network of interrelated archetypal nodes. As in the last chapter's speculation about the way in which scientists in an ordered information universe might see the fundamental particles of their universe, this chapter of her book can be read as an account of a psychologist in an information universe attempting to describe the fundamentals of mind.

Johnstone's Paradox does what some philosophers have always been trying to do: it explains this world in terms of a 'higher world'. The difference is that previous such descriptions have had to look outward from this 'reality' and postulate a supersensible reality whereas Johnstone's Paradox, by invoking artificial intelligence, allows us to look down from the meta-universe and see such ideas from a new perspective.

Now to look at magic itself. A magician performs certain precise ceremonial actions in order to create a required effect. That sentence could equally describe what a scientist does in a practical laboratory demonstration, except we would discourage the emotive word 'ceremonial'. The most obvious difference in the scientist's eyes is that there is a tangible material link between his actions and the resulting effect, whereas the magician seems to think he can produce results without such well-defined links.

As in the case of divination, there are plenty of more or less weak 'scientific' explanations of the way particular magical operations could work. For example: a large part of modern magical practice consists of work on the magician himself, as in a ritual performed to give one courage. In such magic one can argue that the ritual serves to 'hype up' the magician who is performing it, and bring about the required change by psychological means. Similarly with magic that either curses or heals some third party: one can argue that the third party responds psychologically to the knowledge that magic is being done on their behalf. But once again these individual explanations falter when we come to the magic of the New Forest witches who did spells to keep Hitler's army off Britain's shores in the last war - how can a naked dance in Hampshire turn back a U-boat in the North Sea?

The quick answer is that, if we are all part of one universe of ordered information, then we are all intimately linked. Take the human mind as a model of such a 'unified universe' within the human brain, and consider the magician who invokes the goddess Venus in order to win him the heart of the beautiful girl next door. 'How the hell can a myth of ancient Rome exert an influence on a real girl next door?' asks the materialist. The goddess Venus is a concept within the magician's mind, it is a personification of feminine charm, beauty, seductiveness, desirability... The girl next door, as perceived by the magician, is also a concept within the magician's mind; and he happens to be particularly aware of her charm, beauty, seductiveness, desirability...

Now is the materialist seriously trying to tell me that the human brain so utterly squanders its resources that it would hold those two concepts, 'Venus' and 'the girl next door', separately in watertight compartments with absolutely no information overlap and no sharing of brain cells? Such prodigality is to me utterly ridiculous, and utterly out of keeping with natural resourcefulness. I would in fact expect the two concepts to overlap almost entirely if the magician was in love; in computer terms I would expect there to be two files, one containing the information 'Venus is a Roman goddess and X', the other 'Prudence is the girl next door and X' where 'X' in each case calls up a huge common file of details on feminine desirability etc. In these terms there seems nothing at all incongruous to me in invoking Venus in order to woo the girl next door.

Extending the above example to our universe depends on the assumption that it is also a unified 'mind' of ordered information. So when the Hampshire witches held an image in their minds of, let us guess, the old gods of England keeping a German navy from their shores, they were calling up two concepts. One is the old gods of England, whom they will be able to call up only in so far as they have developed a 'sympathy' for them by studying their folklore, looking inward to 'racial memories' etc. As for the German navy, they can invoke this concept only as well as they can picture the types of ship, the typical German sailor, the likely position of those ships at present, and so on. This pictured image of the navy would overlap in some degree with the characteristics of the real German navy - the more clearly and accurately the witches pictured it, the more thoroughly their concept would overlap with the actuality. Similarly, the gods of old England may not be known to the Germans, but it is very likely that they share common ancestry or at least common characteristics with their own gods.

What the witches have done is to bring together these two concepts in a situation where one repels the other. If both concepts exist not only in their brains but also in the great 'brain' that conceives this universe, and if that brain is as well programmed as I suggest our own brains must be, then there is no immediate reason why the old gods of England should not co-operate to keep the actual German navy at bay. The extent to which the operation could actually succeed would depend upon the extent to which the witches had correctly 'invoked' the two concepts - the more thorough the invocation the stronger the link with the actual navy.

As I am wandering far from accepted ideas, a further example is called for. This example also introduces another of the topics that I have grouped under 'magic', namely such spiritual entities as 'angels'. This example describes a magician doing a 'full dress' ceremonial magic ritual in order to clear his flower border of couch grass - an example designed to be illuminating rather than realistic, because most magicians would agree that such an 'earthy' intention as the removing of couch grass would respond far more readily to more humble and 'folksy' types of magic, or even to the use of a spade, than to high kabalistic magic rituals.

Having set up the temple and done the preliminaries, the magician invokes the God (or Goddess) of Nature. Then he invokes the Archangel of the Vegetable Kingdom. Then he invokes the Angel of the Grasses. Then he summons the Spirit of Couch Grass and binds it to obey his will. Then he commands it to clear off his flower border.

I created this very artificial example deliberately to exploit our strong sense of taxonomy in nature: our feeling for the hierarchy of families, species and so on. Imagine that we could recreate all natural phenomena as ordered information, then imagine trying to program a field of grass: millions of individual grass plants, so very much alike and yet each in its own way unique. To start from scratch and program each plant as a totally separate entity would be an unthinkably absurd and uneconomic waste of time and resource. We would almost certainly adopt some sort of hierarchy of files of information as I am about to describe, even if the actual breakdown is quite different or much more complex than the simple description used to illustrate this point.

Each grass plant is a specific example of a particular type of grass plant, a form of living matter. So perhaps we would begin by defining 'living matter', creating a very low level file which encapsulates the essence of living matter, the form of organic molecules, how they build up cells, and all the fundamental properties which distinguish matter that is 'living'. Very likely this program would need to 'call up' (ie include references to) even more fundamental programs which define the basic properties of matter itself. We call this living matter program 'Nature'.

Then we write a program defining the vegetable kingdom. This is a subset of living matter which has certain characteristics which set it apart from animal and insect life. These would be defined and, to save a lot of repetition, this program would call up or refer to the more basic information in the Nature program: we could refer to the 'cells' of vegetation by referring to the previous definition of living cells, rather than having to go into the whole process of re-defining living matter at each reference to it. This program is the Vegetable Kingdom program.

Grass is a particular subset of the vegetable kingdom, with particular properties which define it: for example grass seedlings do not show the two leaves that are common to so many seedlings. We could now write a Grass program which would call up the information which defines a living plant from the Vegetable Kingdom program, and then specify the characteristics which would make it a grass plant.

Now the grass field we want to program is likely to contain many types of grass, each with their own special characteristics. Instead of having to go through all the previous work in each case, we simply create a set of programs, one to each type of grass, and in each program we call up the basic Grass program then add the characteristics which define the specific type of grass. One of those programs will be the Couch Grass program.

Now the field probably contains thousands of couch grass plants; again we do not need to go through all the previous programming for every individual plant. Instead for each couch grass plant we could call up the Couch Grass program and add the characteristics of the individual plant, its size, number of leaves etc. If we were running the program for the whole field, we might have another file containing all the information about the soil and the climatic conditions at every point in the field, and define the plants in this way: so 'Couch 3971' would be the program for the couch plant at location 3971, it would call up the Couch Grass program and input into it the soil conditions, the climatic conditions, plus interaction with other neighbouring plant programs, in order to create the plant which would grow at that point.

If you think all that sounds long-winded, believe me it would be a doddle compared with an attempt to create each plant as an individual entity with no attempt to economise on common information. So my case is that it is scarcely conceivable that something as complex as an ordered information universe could ever be created without considerable economies; and that something akin to this pyramidal programming structure would be expected. Although my explanation was based on the principle 'how would *we* program', the method deduced is fundamental to the way nature works anyway (assuming that the cell structure of a rat in Australia really is similar to that of a rat in London), so it is at least the most natural assumption for humans to make about the way our world could be constructed - and this book is a prediction based upon most natural assumptions.

So how might such a structure be perceived by the inmates of the universe? Surely as just the sort of 'spiritual hierarchy' that was suggested in the ceremonial magician's ritual! Any awareness of these lower level programs would surely give a sense of a 'spirit' that is common to a type - eg the Spirit of Couch Grass, which embodies all that is common to the different couch grass plants, in other words the 'Couch program'. Then an Angel of Grass - a much more abstract entity which embraces all the wide variety of grass forms - ie the Grass program. An Archangel of Vegetation - something so abstract and formless that the mystic would be forced to personify it as a 'Green Giant' or some such form. Then the Nature Goddess Great Isis herself. Be careful not to take these examples of mine too literally, there are many different and overlapping versions of these hierarchies - 'angel' in different systems can cover a wide range of meanings. Probably the 'actual' programming structure is immensely complex, and all traditional hierarchies are merely attempts to clarify the diverse, imperfect visions of this machinery as perceived by merely human mystics.

So the ceremonial magical operation described can be seen as an attempt by the magician to control his reality by gaining access to the lower levels of the software hierarchy, levels which we tend to describe subjectively as 'higher levels'. That makes magic sound so boring, so let's leave it in the usual phrasing: 'the magician attempts to control the world by invoking the spiritual hierarchies'.

That last example got a bit long-winded, so let's quicken the pace a bit.

Ghosts. Again we have weak and inadequate 'semi explanations' which cannot cover all examples.

First that a ghost is totally within the mind of the perceiver: once he has been told there is a ghost he will imagine it. This does not adequately cover the many cases where the perceiver did not know about the existence of a ghost until after he had seen it.

Secondly the idea that a highly charged emotional event can somehow be 'captured' in a physical location, in the sense that a photographic emulsion 'captures' its image. This does not fit the ghosts seen at a distance - eg the ghost of a dead son seen in London at the time that his plane crashed in Africa. Then there is the problem of the haunted house that is demolished, thus removing the physical substance, and a ghost remaining as though associated with the 'location', in the abstract sense, rather than the actual substance of the environment.

These dilemmas would all be resolved in an information universe where information about past occurrences is not deleted, and so all events at any location at any time still 'exist' in the memory of the universe. In view of the fore-mentioned need for economy it would also be unlikely that information ever would be totally deleted, because the destruction of any past programming would require its recreation when similar circumstances arose again: better to store all previous work in modular form and construct future events from past modules. Once the first cell had divided to create a new life, that program should never be rerun but rather retrieved from memory as an effect.

This last point would of course enforce a concept of reincarnation. You know how every teenager who falls in love is the first teenager ever to fall in love, as it were? He experiences the event so vividly, so personally, that he cannot believe anyone else has shared such passion in the past. Wouldn't it be ludicrously uneconomical to create a universe where all that passion really had to be recreated for every spotty romantic throughout history? Much better to run it once as a myth, then run a set of variations on the myth which merely quote the original passion, and then for ever after mankind's romantic experiences will be 'Lego creations' from the basic myths. Of course there will always be new presentations, as these myths are evoked in an evolving world (for example teenagers with cars created the 'Tell Laura I Love Her' romantic myth out of the old kit, and that variation is now available for re-use).

Romance is but one facet of an existence made of so many common experiences. So the idea that we could each be isolated souls, created at birth and totally erased at death, is again totally uneconomical. When a workable character has been evolved in a lifetime, why scrap it when it could be stripped to its essentials and reborn again and again, evolving through every lifetime? Accounts of near-death experiences[22] tally with the idea that our souls are not erased at death.

Telepathy, between people, between animals, and between things. It was recently pointed out that newly discovered chemicals are difficult to crystallize, until someone somewhere has once successfully performed this act. Then it becomes progressively easier all over the world, as if the different batches of that same chemical were somehow telepathically learning from each other how to form crystals. Similarly there is evidence that a trick learned by one creature in one part of the world (for example a rat threading a maze in a psychologist's laboratory) will be learned progressively more quickly by other creatures of the same species - as if they were again learning from each other by telepathy. Similarly it has been suggested that children nowadays will learn to drive cars, or program computers, faster than their parents did, because the human species is itself learning how to do these things.

All these examples, together with individual cases of telepathy between persons, have been debated by scientists, and some have proposed a sort of memory 'field' which links entities of the same species. Such theories are unacceptable to others, because of the basic Aristotelian approach described in the last chapter, which is unwilling to accept explanations based on supersensible causes. But, once again, if our universe is an ordered information universe, then all such telepathy would be not only possible but again highly likely. This is especially true of a field theory which postulates a link between members of a species: the closer you are in type to another being, the closer you are in the software - no matter how distant in physical space. Thus morphic closeness would be more important than spacial closeness in facilitating telepathy.

I do not want this chapter to degenerate into a great rag-bag of examples. Let us practice the economy that I am asking my universe to practice, and summarise my case.

In Chapter 4 (see, I am 'calling up' old arguments rather than re- running them in toto) I spoke of the innate sense of economy in our own thinking, namely 'Occam's Razor'. Occam's Razor is of course an archangel in the same hierarchy as the demon of reductionism. The effect of Occam's Razor has been to exclude nearly all the phenomena of this chapter from serious consideration: why add to the complication of our life by accepting on hearsay evidence a host of strange phenomena like ghosts, clairvoyance etc when so much can be explained by human gullibility? Why clutter our materialist world with a totally unprecedented idea of a 'mind field' linking members of a species, just in order to explain a few statistical irregularities which were probably experimental errors anyway?

Centuries of thinking influenced by Occam's Razor have left us with a very well-shaven world view. So well shaven as to be a bit shiny: what I mean is that if you do start to pile up the evidence for any one phenomenon, then the rationalists react as if this shiny surface was in danger of being broken, and a horde of vagabond concepts were about to storm through the breach.

Assuming there is no immediate revolution in humanity's fundamental thinking processes, we would expect Occam's Razor to remain with us.

So what would be the effect if humanity does begin to believe that our universe might in fact be an 'illusion' created by the ordering of information in a meta-universe? For the sort of economical reasons given above (my Principle of Economy in an information universe being merely an angel in the same hierarchy as the archangel Occam's Razor), we would find it more natural to accept such magical phenomena as ghosts, divination, reincarnation etc, than to reject them. No doubt we would still abuse the word 'logical' as we do now, and protest that it is 'illogical' to think that the positions of the planets could in no way reflect the character of a baby being born at that moment, when we are all part of the same computer program. Reductionism is squeezing our universe into a lifeless lump, a black hole which will implode us into a world of mysticism and magic. Plato is reborn in Aristotle.

I now have a big problem, one of my own creation. At the beginning of this chapter I threatened to lump together a host of unacceptable and outcast ideas to create a 'vagabonds' union' whose combined might could carry enough weight to justify this chapter's existence to the average reader. The danger of a vagabond's union is that it generates tyranny by a simple mechanism: once it has gained a bit of power it uses that power against the establishment, and reduces people who were pillars of society into vagabonds. Thus there are ever more vagabonds to join the union, until a total monopoly is formed. This is described as an illustration of the parallels between the 'real universe' and the information universe I am creating within this book. My vagabond's union has become all powerful and is about to blow my whole structure!

You see, I only wanted to make a 'reasonable case' out of a bunch of outcasts. I wanted this chapter to end with the reader thinking that Johnstone's Paradox and the world of unexplained phenomena were not at variance with each other, but rather they supported each other. But my argument has become too powerful because it has suggested that, as a consequence of a 'connected' universe, every occult or magical phenomenon known to man, becomes not only possible, but practically inevitable!

So now I have to do an about-turn and start explaining why we don't see ghosts all the time, why we don't all remember hundreds of past lives, why everyone is not their own fortune teller, why a horoscope is not a precise, unarguable description of character... indeed why we should have *any* sense of individuality or isolation in such a unified world.

Gulp.

My correct reply is that it is none of my business: this book is merely an attempt to predict how our attitudes to reality are likely to change, so the problems created by that change in attitude will be the business of the scientists and theorists of the future. But I also do not wish the reader to dismiss this prediction too quickly because of certain at present inconceivable consequences. So I will merely try to indicate the directions in which their explanations might evolve.

In Chapter 6 I attempted to visualise the birth of manifestation by seeing it as a cut in nothingness. This idea that a split or 'duality' is a trick at the root of the whole illusion of the world is common to many mystical philosophies. We see it summarised in della Frustas' *Liber Salpinctis Per Tenebras Sonentis*[23] as:

NOTHING

There is no beginning

There was no word

Beyond and throughout the Ever-becoming standeth Vacuum

Behold the surface of a water - is it water? Water it is not. Is it air? Air it is not. Verily the surface is neither air, nor water, for it existeth not excepting that there is some created being to conceive it.

NOTHING IS

It is not, yet we see in it a being. Yea, we see our very selves in reflection. This being, which is not, we name Vacuum.

NOTHING IS NOT

When this nothingness seeketh to explore its nothingness then doth the surface move, curl and seek its own reflection. It reacheth to embrace itself.

CREATION

The wave having broken, nothingness is divided against itself, the surface is a frenzy of foam. Created Being.

UNDERSTANDING

Oh the eternal agony of Vacuum. The endless quest to perceive his nothingness begetteth an endless accident of creation.

Created being standeth apart from Vacuum - yet is all-pervaded by Vacuum. So also the foam is not the surface, yet compriseth an endless division of that surface...

If this illusion of division or duality is the basic archetype of manifestation, then we could expect it to totally pervade manifestation: phenomena would always *seem* to occur in isolation because that is fundamental to the illusion of existence, it is the one principle that stops the universe from imploding back into nothingness. We feel distinct from one another because distinctiveness is our nature, as suggested in Jung's *Septem Sermones Ad Mortuos*[24]. That this illusion of separateness can lead to feelings of impotence, loneliness, and the claustrophobia of the materialist world-view, is a fact which must be balanced against the pleasures of existence, for which it is the price. According to some religions the nadir of separation has been attained, and future progress leads us back to God.

To be a little lower faluting, or should I say 'to falute a little lower'? consider the above example of the teenager in love. If our lives are indeed made up of so many re-enactments of basic archetypal situations or myths, then such a repetitive existence could only enjoy itself by preserving a strict division between its parts. The teenager is the first one ever to fall in love, because that blindness is fundamental to manifest existence: if granted full knowledge of his own tasteless corniness, he would never face the indignity of that plunge into the experience of love, or even of existence.

When we come to creating our own universes we may find that the enormous demands on information storage will enforce the very strictest economies on programming - of the type I have described above. As 'angels' looking down into the worlds of our creation we may feel appalled at the cramped, stereotyped existences that we have created in our 'economy model' universes; and yet the real point will be the fervour and intensity with which those existences are lived by the beings who are born blind to the illusion of their universe. Perhaps creation is a guilty act?

This sense of false isolation which makes our unified universe seem like a chaos of unrelated particles, is the reason that the 'magic' of this chapter has been outlawed. It is also perhaps the reason why God has tended to frown on widespread magical beliefs - many religions oppose magic unless it is firmly in the hands of the priesthood - not wanting the mechanism of this universe to be discovered prematurely, before its lessons had been learned.

Even if the horoscope is the total description of our being, it remains an infernally complex set of interactions to interpret fully. There comes a point in any system of divination when the quest for a precise answer becomes so tedious that it is better to turn our attention back to the original source of the problem... and consider the 'real' world instead!

So let us now leave the subject of magic...

11 Johnstone's Paradox and Society

THIS BOOK IS science fiction - a fact which occurred to me as I wrote the previous chapter.

As a student I used to read a lot of science fiction: it seemed that one of the basic formulae was to notice some trend in society, then to extrapolate that trend to its limits. For example the spread of car ownership would suggest a future society where people lived totally in their cars; the rise of radio would suggest a society of illiterates who saw the written word as subversive. The science fiction writer asks 'what would happen to our world if this or that trend continued unabated, without being diverted by the revolutions and reversals which normally upset the course of history?' The thrill of such books is that they are based on some real present trend, and they predict a horrifying future from which the hero saves mankind in the last chapter.

I have taken the advance of artificial intelligence, and asked what might happen if it continued to advance in the way that its supporters predict. I have suggested how the artists might take up this trend; how the religious leaders might oppose it, until they found unexpected support for their beliefs; how the scientists might find a surprising new angle on the mysteries of matter; and how the occultists and mystics, having been almost squeezed out, will suddenly regain credibility. So what about the horror?

As a science fiction story I should have made much more of the early stages, the claustrophobic squeezing of our world by the reductionist instinct, the loss of magic. Then the Johnstone's Paradox reversal would be the heroic last chapter. This emphasis was achieved in the story of the Minister for Technology and the Pope, but this book as a whole is much more concerned with the after-effects of the revolution. So what difference might it make to our lives, to the society we live in? Is my science fiction story a true horror story?

The answer could form the real justification for this whole book, because I think that the revolution I predict will have profound consequences, consequences which will extend well beyond the resolution of certain hoary philosophical riddles. I also see those consequences being very beneficial for society.

In Chapter 2 I suggested that knowing too much about our world was killing our world, because our knowledge was shrinking it. In the fifties we looked forward to discovering life on Mars; now we know there is none. In Chapter 9, mind you, this anti-knowledge stance was qualified: it is the reductionist instinct which Aristotelian method seems to evoke, which causes the world to shrink, while there is another type of knowledge which actually increases the world.

There is a social analogy of this process. The greater the flow of information about current affairs, the more helpless we begin to feel. Although we might expect our knowledge of the world to increase our sense of potential and give us all greater hope, in practice it so often makes us merely feel inadequate, insignificant and despairing. Just as the 'demon' of reductionism makes us see the advance of scientific knowledge as a shrinking of our universe, so does a similar demon poison our perception of society: when we watch a film about the American plutocracy we do not rejoice to think that one day we might enjoy such a life style, instead we lament the gulf that separates us from such affluence.

If I was a blacksmith's son in a mediaeval village, my life would offer far fewer choices than there are for members of our society; but in relative terms there was greater scope for fulfillment than for most of us. The relativity I speak of is the relativity between our dreams and our possible achievements. That blacksmith's son can become *the* blacksmith for his village. He can compete for trade in the limited field of the neighbouring villages and extend his reputation to proportions which seem heroic to a population that never travels further than the next valley. He can be the *Victor Ludorum* in the village games, he can forge a new wrought-iron gate for the church and know it will be used for centuries to come.

The equivalent young person today can hardly expect such significance. The most significant thing to aspire to is to be an influential pop star, but as soon as one looks at the possibility one finds millions of young hopefuls in a rat-race for a few golden thrones. They all want to be King, because the flow of information has told them so much about their heroes: they know that they began as humble kids like themselves, that they started in gigs at school like themselves. That blacksmith's son never expects to be King, because his King lives in a different world.

Intimate secrets of the famous in the newspapers, and the private lives of the folk in *Dynasty* on television, tell us that the few positions of privilege are filled with ordinary humans like ourselves, or worse than ourselves, who have been blessed with better fortune than we will ever have. Even a million-pound pools win, the only hope for most of us, would not go far in *Dallas*.

For the purpose of this book we do not want to glamorise the life of the blacksmith's son. His is the happiness of ignorance, and it is contrasted with the dissatisfaction born of knowledge - which is itself a form of progress. But, as suggested at the beginning of this chapter, progress in any straight line leads to horror. It is the twists and revolutions along the way (the turbulence in time described in Chapter 7) that save from horror and turn progress into evolution. The difference now is that we see so far, and that merely tells us how much farther we have to go.

The worst aspect of this dissatisfaction lies in our relationship with authority. Seeing ourselves as a particle in a vast sea of less fortunate beings makes it hard to accept the government of the few lucky ones in power, especially when the flow of information keeps us aware of their human weaknesses. 'Why should that bitch Thatcher be able to step in and make us all unemployed?'; 'Just because Reagan is already half dead does not mean he has the right to risk the destruction of the whole world in nuclear holocaust'. What can the frustrated individual on the dole do when the DHSS expects him to queue for hours only to be insulted by a man behind a bullet-proof plastic grille?

A major ingredient in this sense of hopelessness is the un-connected view of the world tackled in the last chapter. We see ourselves as drops in an ocean, where previous generations in the industrial age saw themselves as cogs in a machine. The drop in the ocean has greater freedom of motion, but has infinitesimal value. The cog in the machine is caught in the structure, but at least knows that the whole machine depends critically on its existence. What is needed for progress is a view which gives that sense of value, but without denying the sense of individuality.

The realisation that one might be part of a great information universe - a program in the software of that universe - can provide that better view, because it preserves the best points of both the 'drop in the ocean' and the 'cog in the machine' concepts. The drop of water has individuality on its own, it is a microcosm of the ocean itself; but it loses all value when dropped into the ocean. The cog has no such individuality: without the machine it is dead, but at least it knows that without the cog the machine is also dead. A program is like a cog in that it gains extra value by being part of a larger program, but it is also like the drop of water in that it is a program in its own right - a microcosm of the greater program.

So, although it might at first seem a repulsive to view oneself as a program within the software of the universe, the more one considers the idea the more it can give purpose and meaning to ones' life, without destroying our new found sense of individuality. It gives every one of us significance and potential. The lonely meditator in the Himalayas, or in a Brixton bedsit, is as close to the software of this universe as is the president of the United States. In fact, because the 'Famous' are mostly caught up in the 'rut' of success, the lonely failure is potentially closer to reality, for it is surely the dreams of the non-entities which inflate the famous - the stars are caught up in the dreams of the common people, and often cannot escape them.

That blacksmith's son knows kingship: he experiences it when he wins the pig in the village wrestling match. But when we win such an honour at our village fete we know, having seen the 'real champions' on telly, that the prize we win is but a token or toy. People of limited imagination know kingship when they become president of their local Bus-shelter Preservation Group. Such people become petty tyrants in a post which most people would either avoid, or merely accept from a sense of duty, because further-sighted folk appreciate the ultimate insignificance of that position in the greater context of this world.

But in an information universe those whose imagination is too far-sighted to be content with petty honours would learn to realise that the archetype of kingship is all-pervasive; that the spirit of kingship can be invoked in a humble local capacity just as well as it can when one is Prime Minister. Such realisation would tend to de-fuse the 'them and us' feeling and bring about a practical understanding of the extent to which kingship is in practice a form of slavery. The real potential lies not with a harassed politician (who has sacrificed his human potential to become a mouthpiece for some evolving political theory), but rather with the meditator in the Brixton bedsit - once the enormous step of realising that potential has been made.

Consider again the frustrated would-be pop star. In the separatist materialist world-view he is someone who is born unlucky, for he does not 'contain' the talent of a super-star like Bob Dylan. But in an information universe the talent seems less like a personal property: Bob Dylan is seen as a medium, a mouthpiece for a spirit which swept across the world in the sixties. The reason he became famous was because his records sold, and the reason they sold was because we liked them, and the reason we liked them was because the spirit that spoke through his songs was also present in our hearts. So we were all participants in his success, not talentless failures grovelling in the dust about his feet.

So the first benefit from Johnstone's Paradox could be the sense that we all, every one of us, *matter*. And that the keys of the universe are as accessible to a poor student as they are to the Principal in charge of a multi-million pound high energy physics project. This sense of worth is analogous to the sense of meaning which the near-death experience gives to those who have experienced it[25].

With this sense of self worth goes the realisation that our principles also matter: morality is no longer in official hands, instead it comes home to roost in the individual.

Let us say that you are passionately opposed to the wholesale destruction of trees to produce trivial paper luxuries (such as this book). Then you could make sure that you never waste paper, that you always remove your paper from other trash and leave it bundled separately for the dustmen to collect. This is very worthy, but unfortunately a lot of local councils cannot cope with the separate collection of paper waste, so it all gets thrown in the same tip despite your efforts. It is therefore natural to feel impotent, to feel that 'The System' is against you, and so to give up the pointless exercise of separating out paper that is never going to be recycled anyway. This is, however, very bad for one's soul! When conscience urges a certain action, but despair or hopelessness over-rides that call to action, then in most people the original impulse seems to turn to bitterness and poison. In an unconnected universe it is not easy to justify some of our moral feelings: the sense of being mere drops in an ocean destroys all the value of what are merely token actions of conscience.

But when we see ourselves as part of an information universe, then the 'connectedness' described in the last chapter comes into play. As a symbolic gesture, separating out our waste-paper does have value: it is an act of ritual magic, it is a confirmation of intent. By reinforcing daily this dedication to the cause, we are imprinting it on the software of our species: others will become conscious of the need to save paper, a groundswell of public opinion is being fostered by our private but single minded action. One could even take the magical view and argue that the Tree Gods themselves will bless you for your endeavours on their behalf. Indeed, merely by the act of acknowledging to ourselves that we have moral principles we may be benefiting mankind as a whole. By giving value to such moral principles, Johnstone's Paradox gives value to each one of us.

There is a further important consequence of Johnstone's Paradox: the recognition that living beings are composed of ordered information, goes hand in hand with the recognition that ordered information can itself become a living entity.

The disgusting treatment that the bureaucracy, or big business, inflicts upon people invokes an anger that is otherwise in danger of being expressed against bureaucrats or businessmen - a confusion of the entity with the individuals working within it. Society becomes divided against itself. Johnstone's Paradox can bring about a real feeling for something that otherwise remains in the rarified intellectual atmosphere of 'obvious truths', namely that a belief or 'system' can develop an autonomous intelligence which is usually of a fairly low order, and is not ultimately dedicated to serving humanity so much as ensuring its own survival.

For example: we all realise that the Inland Revenue is the vilest cancer on earth, with no redeeming feature that has not been paid for a hundred times over with human misery, extortion, corruption and terrorism. Yet some quite pleasant people work there, and hang on to their source of income by closing their eyes and imagining it is all in a good cause. Yet it is very hard for the rest of Britain to believe that decent humans could crawl into such a poisoned sewer of moral degradation. It is hard for us to accept that there is any room for good intention within that putrid, gangrenous sore in the flesh of society - just as it must have been hard for Jews under the holocaust to appreciate the earnest endeavours of the Waffen SS to purify and cleanse the Great German Nation...

If I expand on this topic it is just conceivable that I might risk losing my pristine academic objectivity. Suffice it to say that it is very healthy to be able to draw a distinction between the cancer of taxation and the poor enslaved humans who feed its growth. Indeed it is healthy to be able to draw a clear distinction between the 'spirit' or living intelligence of any system or ideology, and the people whom it involves in its cause.

This ability, to draw a distinction between an obsessive idea and the person in whom it is resident, is a useful mechanism which society loses when it abandons the idea of 'demonic possession'. We are inclined to become polarised against people who advocate extreme ideas - so much so that we are forced to the opposite extreme ourselves, and become part of the same obsession. In the past we might simply have recognised that those people were demonically possessed.

Do you know someone who has had a breakdown and come out of it a 'born again Christian'? You feel glad to see them back on their feet after their crisis, but find that you can no longer talk to them? Whenever you make conversation, you find it is not the person that now speaks, but rather an obsession? Something human seems to have been pushed out?

The same thing can happen with political conversion, or with someone who goes overboard on a new psychological theory or a new guru. What is happening is that an idea is behaving as a demon. Information does not need to be structured into a material institutions like a civil service in order to be manifest as a living entity, it can simply exist as lower level software of our universe.

If you can accept the idea that ordered information within a great 'computer' could think and see itself as a living person going about life in what, to us, is an 'inner world', in that case what would be the status of an information complex like 'freedom', or 'individualism', or 'Marxism'? It would not be manifest in that inner world as a living being, because it is just an idea and has no input from the biological software of the inner world. On the other hand the idea would have an input into the person's mind - the person probably perceives it as 'an abstract idea that has no existence except as part of my mind'. But we, as outsiders to his inner world, know that the idea is another program of information in the software, existing in its own right, interacting with other programs of which the person's mind is but one example. In effect, it is what one might call a 'demon' or a 'god' or a 'spirit'... depending on your own subjective awareness of that program.

In the 'Magic' chapter I presented a very formal model of this idea of demons and angels: here I am re-presenting it without the hierarchical structure and pointing out that every abstract idea, named or un-named, has the potential to operate as a disembodied, autonomous being which can interact with human minds. Sometimes the results are pleasing, and sometimes they are not.

The effect is similar to a virus. I gather that a virus is like a fragment of DNA coded with alien information: when it enters a living cell, the information in the virus becomes incorporated into the host DNA and starts to reproduce itself. Think of Thatcherism, Stalinism, Fundamentalism and such nasties in the same light: they are names we have given for packets of information once semi-dormant in the software of our universe but which have mutated to a form in which they can enter the programs of human minds and start reproducing themselves. Most important of all: recognise that it is not necessary to like a demon to serve it, those who become obsessed by Thatcherism can best spread the disease by hating it in public. Try it. (No, try it on my ideas, please!)

Understanding gods and demons can explain a lot about the paradoxes of kingship. What do weak people mean when they demand 'strong government'? Adolf Hitler is the epitome of the strong leader, in those terms, yet psychologically he is seen as a weak personality that was open to obsession. Stanley Baldwin was so strong in his common sense that he did not appear to recognise and make allowance for the weakness of those who would succumb to the god of war.

Jung wrote, in his *Septem Sermones Ad Mortuos*[26] that 'the gods are many, whilst men are few', and that 'numberless gods await the human state'. It seems the ultimate purpose of all information in the software of this universe is that it should be manifest as phenomenon. The shortcut to that manifestation is to use a human mind as a medium. That is why our lives are a constant battleground of conflicting ideas grappling to usurp our consciousness. In Chapter 13 I present a model where we experience two classes of 'gods': there are the complexes of information within the software of our own universe, as described here, and there are also conscious minds attempting to interact with us from outside our universe - the possibilities are endless!

A human mind is a masterpiece of flexible adaptability: you can test that it is in gear by changing it. I have met many 'single minded' people in my life, but in each case the single mind I spoke to was not their own one.

We saw an example of demonic possession recently: terrorism is another movement which has grown to become a force in the world. Basically a political method (though those who wish to whitewash politics would call it 'anti-political'), terrorism has fed upon the social equivalent of psychic energy to become a major demon - publicity feeds terrorism, terrorism raises publicity. As long as terrorism is 'out there', or something that only happens to other people, then its power is limited. But when those in no immediate danger from it suddenly become passionately involved in 'the battle against terrorism' then you know they have themselves become possessed by the demon. This is very obvious, but only to those not so possessed: what they can see is that the possessed ones no longer recognise terrorism as an abstract entity, instead the label is projected onto real humans. They will then bomb Tripoli as a 'blow against terrorism', not recognising that the bombing of civilians in peacetime in order to de-stabilise a hated regime is nothing other than an act of terrorism - it was the demon which had its finger on the trigger, not a human. Such possessed people will turn on those who have resisted possession and cry that they are cowards who are not prepared to make a stand against terrorism. Unfortunately, unless those accused fully understand the symptoms and can accept the reality of demonic possession, then they are liable to feel ashamed and be swept up in the group madness.

Painful examples of such possessions abound. The Nazis, who longed to sweep Germany clean, lost sight of the real malaise and focussed on people as victims; as a result they became the embodiment of the sickness that they had originally sensed in German society. The hawks in the Kremlin arm Russia to the teeth in order to keep at bay the oppression and tyranny over workers that they see in the capitalist system; but they have greatly 'improved upon' that tyranny themselves. The Southern States 'redneck' keeps his rifle loaded and dreams of a chance to blow apart the vile corrupting disease of communist subversion; but, if he overlooked the labels and accepted the reality, that redneck would find himself much more at home in the puritan Soviet lifestyle than in the liberal society which he believes he is defending.

It is most instructive of all to look at examples close to home. I remember a Times article which spoke of the need to strengthen ourselves against the influence of Soviet subversion which pervaded the CND and so many other western institutions. They described the Russian government as a mighty totalitarian force that was dedicated to world domination. The strange thing was that the whole piece was itself an unconscious paean of praise to totalitarianism. The first thing we learned was that totalitarianism is reliable: some past statement by a Soviet leader (that they were committed to enforcing the benefits of their lovely political system on the rest of the world) was accepted as gospel truth and assumed to be still universally true. It was never considered that politics could have tainted the veracity of this statement; that it might have been originally conjured up to keep some internal Soviet hawks quiet. Such unwavering communist commitment to a principle over so many years contrasted very favourably with our politicians: when the Conservatives say they intend to reduce unemployment we all fall about laughing! No-one remembers a western politician's promises for more than a week, yet statements from behind the Iron Curtain are cherished and quoted back for decades. So the first unconscious message from that article was this: when a totalitarian regime utters a statement you don't like, at least you can be sure it is true - something you can never be sure of with democratic politicians.

Next this article told us how efficient and effective totalitarianism is compared to western governments which cannot even rule their own members, let alone their own countries. The Soviet government is apparently not only able to keep all of its vast population under tight control, it also runs several other countries with equal precision; what is more it is apparently running most of our own left-wing institutions, so skillfully that our gullible liberals do not even realise they are being ruled from Moscow. (Blimey, if the Soviet system is that competent we ought not to be resisting it, we ought to be begging it to take over the rest of the world!) One can imagine the unconscious effect of reading articles like this at a time when the competence of democracy is under scrutiny. The conscious message of the piece - that Russia is evil - is so simple and seductive that it causes the reader to lap up the subliminal message which is that totalitarianism is the only really efficient and workable system if you want law and order. It is this unconscious message or 'demon' which then pulls the strings, making the reader think that it would be a good idea to abolish trade unions and increase our military power to Soviet levels in order to keep this evil at bay. In other words we should become totalitarian in order to save us from totalitarianism. Present this analysis to someone already possessed by this demon and they will not look at the overall message I am describing, instead they will vigorously defend individual statements within such an article and accuse you of being a communist yourself.

That example was rather laboured because overexposure to the media can numb our awareness of the double standards in so much political argument. Looking at one such blatant example illustrates the point so that the reader can look out for other examples of the way that beliefs or systems will enslave people and spread their influence independently of any nominal political grouping.

Most people imagine that Naziism was defeated in 1945: that is like believing that the disease anthrax has died when the afflicted elephant finally expires - now we can celebrate by eating the flesh of the corpse! It is worth considering how many ('good' as well as 'bad') Nazi dreams have been realised since that date: the restoration of German economic power, racism, the people's car, guided missiles, the motorway system, the universal propaganda...

The understanding that one's real enemy is often a belief or system, rather than other people, is the greatest step towards liberation. My reaction to that original talk on machine intelligence could so well have been one of anger at the presumption of such scientists. I could have become a loony campaigner against the 'scientific establishment' (rather than a loony campaigner for a half-baked theory called 'Johnstone's Paradox').

The revolution I am describing is one which could at last reveal to man who his true enemies are: not fellow men so much as the ideologies and delusions which used to be called 'demons'. Effective action against, say, vandalism is only really possible when we have put aside the dreadful seduction of concentrating our rage on vandals. Only when we fully understand how a nation of reasonably lovable people can evoke a bastard national policy, have we any real hope of achieving lasting peace with that nation. Only when we have evoked the Spirit of War in our own souls will we be able to see how peace could be everlasting without being boring. Until that time we do not really want peace.

Johnstone's Paradox could alter our views of warriorship. Enmity is a very intimate relationship, second only to marriage. To occupy yourself with an enemy you despise is as foolish and degrading as it is to marry a partner you do not respect. Before battle we should study our opponents until we reach a level of respect which borders on love: then we are ready for battle. Such conflict can actually ennoble both parties, because there is less risk of obsession in it, whereas battles fuelled by contempt and hatred are battles where *both* parties will usually be defeated by the same presiding evil principle. We set out once to fight fascism in the shape of Nazi Germany, and yet the long term result was a triumph for fascist principles. What government does not now believe that the real essentials for survival are superior firepower, ruthlessness, and above all better propaganda?

Johnstone's Paradox will soften the distinction between humans and the machines we create; and this will allow us to see the distinction more realistically. It will allow us to see how the individual fits into a system, which can become an extension of his being.

At the gut level we already sense this: we feel that the car we drive is an extension of our body and much of the bad feeling between motorists is ascribed to the sense of extended territory which is felt by the car driver. But, because we also hold at the gut level a belief that we are fundamentally superior to 'mere machines' we do not fully acknowledge the extent to which the car is an extension of our body, and we are puzzled by our own behaviour. We know that brain size is not the sole determinant of intelligence, that relative size is an important factor (the elephant is less intelligent than a human, despite his sizable brain), but we find it difficult to relate this to the way that machinery enlarges our own bodies. When a driver becomes identified with his vehicle, his brain is being 'diluted' in a larger body, and it is not surprising that the combined system should show signs of regression to a lower order of intelligence. The bigger the car, the more primitive the beast; and when we send our soldiers to war in lumbering tanks and mighty fighter aircraft we are not sending out rational human beings to act on our behalf.

By clarifying our relationship to machinery, Johnstone's Paradox could help us to understand how we interact with it. We will no longer feel perplexed by the way technology seems to 'take us over'. Instead of seeming like an alien force invading our lives, technology will look more like a welcome marriage partner. Weird sex!

So the future I am predicting is not a horrific one. Although we might initially recoil from the idea that we are programs in the software of reality, once we have grown out of our tendency to see this in reductionist terms the idea could eventually do much to restore our individual sense of worth. By restoring our sense of mystery, as suggested in the last chapter, it could reverse the sense of claustrophobia that reductionism engenders, as discussed in Chapter 2. And until that sense of spiritual claustrophobia is tackled there can be no real solution to the 'problem' that society has made of drug taking, for example.

The Paradox could also engender a new moral impulse, in the sense of a genuine awareness of our own ethical feelings as opposed to 'morality' which means slavish dedication to some written law. By increasing our awareness of the more subtle forces which rule our lives, this principle could begin to free us from their tyranny, and reduce the human bloodshed that they demand. Who knows, we might even get rid of the Inland Revenue...

Pretty good value from a little paperback book, don't you reckon? Any other problems I can sort out while I'm at it?

Vote, vote, vote for Johnstone's Paradox. Just don't get too enthusiastic about it, please!

12
Johnstone's Paradox and Us

We have explored the paradox shallowly in a wide variety of contexts, in each case looking at a range of examples. The examples chosen have been suggestive rather than comprehensive - the idea is to encourage others to continue this exploration. In the terms of Chapter 6 we have used a mixture of the philosophical, the academic and the imaginative methods. The vivid approach is another matter; you could say it requires practical demonstration, that it really lies outside the scope of a mere book. But I did promise to return to it later.

This book began by looking at those books of liberating ideas which emerge to brighten our world briefly before being doused in a flood of negative evidence or criticism. I suggested that they served a useful purpose (as well as earning a possible fortune for their authors), and that I wished to attempt such a book myself.

The great value of such books lies (for the reader) in the relief they give from the boring predictability of this world: wouldn't it be just terrific if a flying saucer from Venus landed in Hyde Park and forced the scientific establishment to eat its words? (Actually it would also be likely to have a disrupting effect on society by scaring people silly.) So these books are an antidote to the claustrophobia of reductionism, to the tendency to reduce the best things in this world to 'nothing but'. As their effect seems fairly short-lived in the public field, we can consider them to be a sort of morphine jab to relieve the pain of possession by the reductionist demon.

After the examples of possession by political demons in the last chapter, we should be able to recognise the paradoxical symptoms of possession by the reductionist demon. Basically it shows as an exaggerated anger against scientists, and against technology, and a corresponding clutching at any new theory which looks like blowing them apart. This last fact illustrates the sort of close relationship you can expect between a demon and its polar opposite: in this case the polar opposite is the claustrophobic desire to expand our reality.

If my prescription is right, then I should try to extend the anaesthetic effect it offers. So this book contains hardly a single scrap of evidence to support its predictions, for evidence is fatal in these books when the reductionist demon lurks at the back of the reader's mind, waiting to strike back. Such a reader only has to find a single flaw in the evidence or a single reviewer critical of the book's academic respectability, and the book is thrown down in disgust as 'nothing but' a hoax, or another crank theory, or whatever. The reductionist demon has reclaimed his territory in the reader's mind. So with this book I made sure the demon would have to wait while you go out to find your own evidence.

Similarly there is a lack of tight logical argument in the book. If it appears otherwise at times, it is simply that the author knows his logic and can choose to sail quite close to the wind. But, in general, arguments have done their best to pull themselves up by their own bootstraps, even when those bootstraps have been long enough to wrap themselves around a few other arguments along the way. It is therefore necessary for the readers to do their own logical exploration of the theme... while the reductionist demon waits and curses impatiently.

In the sense that this book, like any book, is an initiatory journey, it is worth noting that the archetypal initiatory journey which tradition tells us is symbolised in the 22 trump cards of the tarot pack, is a journey which begins not with the High Priest or the Emperor, but with the Fool, and the Juggler or street magician. My attitude to evidence is therefore that of the Fool, and my reasoning is that of the con-man with the wand. There was another chapter I felt tempted to write for this book, but omitted it because it was the only one that I was academically qualified to write, and so out of keeping with the spirit of the whole. I believe that ignorance is also a path.

As for the street magician - are you prepared for him on the initiatory path? When he does a few conjuring tricks then sells you some hair restorer which really does cure your baldness, how do you then react when the local chemist analyses the restorer and says that you have spent good money on a bottle of sea water with no active ingredient? Do you worry your hair out again with anger, or do you rejoice in your triple bargain, a single purchase which gave three great gifts: a cure for baldness, a revelation of the psychosomatic foundations of the affliction, plus a great lesson about con men?

If you do continue to explore the theme of this book, it makes a big difference how you go about it; because the vivid approach is almost bound to play its part in any first-hand exploration, and the vivid approach requires one to adopt an attitude, and live within it. This is why the vivid approach is a little offensive to the philosophical, and to the academical mentalities. The philosophical approach really does require one not to take sides, whereas the academic approach is in fact quite impractical unless you do take sides while researching, but it is nevertheless vital that the traces of this bias are kicked over in the summing up.

What critics of the vivid approach do not realise, presumably because they have never done it consciously, is the extent to which one can 'believe in' or commit oneself for or against a theory without actually succumbing to it. This is one of those traditional 'secrets' of magic which no-one needs to keep secret in the ordinary sense; it can be shouted from the rooftops because it is a secret that protects itself by being difficult to master.

The ability to read a horoscope in depth, or to invoke Venus to improve one's love life, does correlate with the extent to which you believe in their efficacy. Examples of rationalist sceptics who have been dumbfounded into accepting magic usually turn out to be people for whom scepticism was only a thin line of defence against a naturally superstitious nature. For practicing magicians, belief is a quantitative thing - they can believe in something just enough to get it to work, but not enough to want to convince anyone else - and so they tend to gag on the sceptic's question 'do you *really* believe in spirits?'.

Questions like that reveal that for the rationalist, as for the religious person, belief seems to be a binary on/off effect.

I especially need to labour this description of the vivid approach when writing for an English audience, because it is something that the English find more difficult. Perhaps because the English have raised acting to a Great Art, they are correspondingly not very good at applying acting in everyday life: they believe too much in the existence of objective truth to be much good at behaving 'as if' things were true.

For example: English businessmen are less competent marketers than, say, Americans. They will hold up their marketing decisions for months, endlessly re-working the concept and re-writing the advertisements, because there is an unconscious belief that out there exists one perfect, unique, absolute way to sell their product, and if they keep working at it they will eventually find it - whereas they often end up with a rather tired and costly compromise. American businessmen, on the other hand, are better able to throw themselves into a second rate promotion and bring the whole thing to life simply by believing in it.

The act of behaving 'as if' something is true, the ability to offer a measure of belief as a sort of sacrificial libation to an idea, is what distinguishes the vivid approach. As was mentioned in Chapter 6, the vivid approach is in a sense the 'magical' approach: so perhaps we had better kick off with a magic ritual to make it seem authentic!

Go into an empty room by yourself. The room should be quiet and still. Light an incense stick and seat yourself comfortably about a yard away from the incense: a distance which allows you to watch it burning without disturbing it too much with your own breath. Relax, slow your breath so as to make the mind reasonably calm, and watch the smoke curling up from the incense stick.

You will observe that it creates lovely shapes, an exquisite ever-changing dance of filmy coils and fluttering veils: just as an angel or fairy cloak should be, if only angels and fairies really existed. Allow yourself to see this beauty, to experience it. The full experience of this beauty probably involves casting off the 'realisation' that it is 'only smoke'.

Now ask yourself why this is happening, why the smoke does not just go straight up to the ceiling then spread out as a flat sheet. Realise that you are seeing the effect of tiny air currents, and that these currents are themselves not straight flows of air, but dancing vortices and fluttering veils: the smoke is simply revealing movements that already exist in the air. It is reacting to the greater macro-currents as well as to the all-pervasive and continual micro-collisions of the molecules of air in the room. The latter explain why the smell of the incense, just like any other smell, will pervade all quarters of the room within seconds.

Realise that these currents and these constant bombardments add up to a colossal interchange and flow of information throughout the room. Every whirl and vortex that you can see is shaped according to the most complex equations of fluid dynamics for a compressible medium, that it is just an overview of a hugely more complex molecular 'game of billiards' beyond the reach of your eyesight, and that this one vortex just happens to be a one visible example of the patterns dancing invisibly throughout the entire volume of the room.

When you have a good feeling of this great dance of information, realise that it is happening faster, in a more complex fashion, and through a much greater volume than the comparatively sluggish information exchanges going on within the liquid and solid structures of your own brain. The air in the room is like a great living thing, an airy spirit of immense speed and subtlety, and it contains you and nourishes you. If that thought frightens you, then remember that fear alters the chemical balance in your body and alters the smell of your sweat in a way which animal noses can detect. That smell will be transmitted throughout the room in seconds: the room will 'know' you are scared and it will convey this information via draughts to the world outside.

When this sense of the living reality of the room is strong, extend it to a realisation that the empty room which contains you is just a speck in a complex universe. For all its enormous complexity, the room was something that you deliberately chose for its comparative simplicity and peacefulness, so as not to be distracted in the meditation.

When the sense of the universe as a living whole grows strong, then return to your own mind and appreciate that there has been nothing in the whole meditation that has not been perceived by, modelled, and examined within the structure of your own brain and thought processes. There was nothing described that could not be reduced to the basic laws of physics: simplicity in combination begets complexity of experience.

A supporting meditation is to contemplate the surface of a river or stream; to realise that the surface is purely a boundary between two states, and that it is receptive to both states - currents of air and of deeper water - and responds to them both, as well as it mirrors the light that shines on the surface - which light being the medium that transmits the information back to you. Feel the surface to be a living skin, and listen to the ripples of water around a rock or obstruction. Think of its turbulent flow as a complex fluidic system with its own 'mind'. Normally we listen to water as an overall sound; try instead to listen to it as one would to a roomful of people, or as a musician would listen to a symphony: that is to say listen for the separate 'voices' within the whole sound and try to follow them. What is this living thing trying to tell you? Is it literal information as in conversation, or aesthetic as in music?

This latter meditation can be supplemented by reading a book called *Sensitive Chaos* [27] which is about water as a living structure. Another book to read, though it would be better to see an exhibition of its content in action, is *Kymatics* [28]. This shows how fine powder, for example, when subjected to sound can form patterns which not only look astonishingly similar to the structure of living cells, but they are in fact dynamic structures within which the particles flow along ordered tracks. Meditating on these 'living patterns' of 'dead particles' dancing to sound waves, it is comparatively easy to soften the rigid distinction between what is dead and what is alive, between inanimate matter and living cells.

These meditations all serve that same purpose. As was explained in Chapter 2, one of the processes of reductionism is that it moves forward like a bulldozer, squeezing 'life' out of existence: first we learn that rocks are not alive, then that plants are 'purely mechanical', then animals, and then us. By softening the blade of that bulldozer in these meditations, we are able to move back against its passage as described in Chapter 2, spreading life back down the chain until we see the whole universe as a vast living entity - mechanism ceases to be a demon and becomes instead an angel. Instead of love being 'nothing but' a chemical reaction, we begin to see even chemical reactions as an expression of all-pervasive love - more of a fun idea.

According to tradition you should keep a close written record of your progress with such meditations: this record will then preserve accounts of 'miracles' or altered states of consciousness, the memory of which is otherwise liable to be erased by the weight of everyday experience.

To obtain greater freedom of belief it is necessary to soften the rigid boundaries of your 'real' beliefs. Perhaps this book is irritating to you, because you 'know' that matter is matter, religion is only a useful psychological myth, whereas magic is a useless myth and so rubbish; or perhaps, by way of contrast, you 'know' that a loving creator made this world, or that matter is a great sea of etheric vibrations, and so you are irritated by a book which seems to accept that 'mere machines' could imitate such divine processes. In either case these meditations could soften those hard distinctions and open up greater possibilities: in the first case possibilities for more mystery, and in the second for greater technical achievements by humanity.

Once it is possible to begin to at least kid yourself this could be a universe of ordered information, start to live in it. When you walk down a street your eyes are presented by a continuously changing perspective, every visible object slides across your field of vision in a precise geometrical relationship to reinforce the illusion that one is really moving through three-dimensional space. Creating this illusion in video graphics takes a lot of programming so, rather than ignoring the phenomenon because you know it is 'bound' to happen because you 'really are' walking in three dimensional space, instead rejoice in this masterpiece of precision and see if you can catch it out - see if you can see any errors in the programming which cause the odd visual quirk. Joel Biroco describes a similar meditation[29] of imagining while walking that you are remaining stationary and the universe is being moved around you, like a sophisticated back projection system.

Similarly, you can test the universe's memory function by leaving some object in a place where it won't be disturbed. Return from time to time to see if it is still there exactly as you left it. If it is not, appreciate how even the best computer can occasionally misplace information. Examine your bank statements closely and note how perfectly it all adds up and is held in the computer's memory. If you find the odd error, understand that it is just the odd error. Keep track on the contents of your purse or wallet too. If money which should be there is suddenly missing accept that it is just an odd hiccup in the program, rather than trying to explain away the loss. See if you can manipulate these hiccups in your favour to produce occasional pleasant surprises when you open your wallet. There is one traditional way of tampering with the software; it involves rotating one's money at the time of the New Moon; find out and experiment - if it does not work be thankful that the universe's software is so tamper-proof.

Experiment also with rituals of communion. If you are separated from, say, someone you love, and you meditate upon them, then the popular expression is that you are 'with them in your thoughts'. Do you feel close to them? As two members of the same species you would expect to be close neighbours in the software of the universe - as explained in Chapter 10. By thinking about the person you will become even closer, because more programs will be common to you both. If you go a stage further and plan to both perform a ritual of communion - for example to both light a candle at midnight and think of each other simultaneously - then you will be even closer in the software, no matter how many miles separate you in space. That is because you are not only members of the same species, you are also performing a similar action with similar intent at the same moment. Extending this idea: if a whole brotherhood decides to light a candle with common intent at the same time, then you are coming together in the software of the universe no matter how scattered you are on the surface of the earth. One would expect such a 'meeting of souls' to be every bit as effective as a physical meeting. On this point it is worth considering what happens when people think they are doing the ritual at the same moment, but in fact are not - because of differences in time zones or of a clock that is wrong. The relative efficacy of the resulting ritual could provide a measure of the relative importance of objective and subjective time in the software of the universe.

Recognise the signs of demonic possession by ideas - in yourself and in others. If you find that you become infuriated and helpless-feeling in the face of some creed or craze, then the chances are that it has a hold on you just as much as if you embraced it. Think of it as a demon or 'idea virus' in your mind instead of ranting about it in public, and see if you can destroy it by analysis of its hold on you. Then you will be able to resist spreading the virus by infecting others. There is nothing glamorous about pacifism, Thatcherism, Marxism or any otherism except the anger of their opponents.

Encourage also your ability to recognise the signs of 'mind' within systems, to be able to distinguish between the apparent evil intentions of an institution and the innocence of the people involved in it. Because the mouthpieces for bureaucracy tend to be mature adults, it is hard to accept that they are acting for a group mind which is at best infantile, but more likely subhuman. Next time you get caught in a bureaucratic nightmare, restrain your wholesome, natural instinct to direct a fire-hose of concentrated nitric acid through the hole in the grille on to the people in the office beyond. Instead, look at the system as a living entity and ask yourself what is it trying to tell you? If a delinquent child behaved as badly as the civil service, what sort of cry from the heart might it be trying to convey? What is it like and how might you yourself react to feeling rejected? Would you refuse to treat that child as a whole, but rather punch him in the mouth? When you have decided the answer, set up that fire hose...

Above all, use your own ingenuity to extend, adapt and build on all these exercises. Their long term aim is to invoke a feeling for the oneness of the universe. Many people nowadays have cultivated this feeling of being part of the whole, but in many cases this feeling has been realised by a process of rejecting the logic of science - by turning one's back on accepted views of reality and assuming that we are all part of God, or made up of etheric vibrations, or whatever.

The difference here is that we are reaching a sense of the wholeness of the universe not by rejecting the analytical, materialistic world-view but rather by carrying it to its 'logical' conclusion in the form of Johnstone's Paradox - reaching toward a holistic world-view but without sacrificing logic - and then encouraging emotional acceptance of the idea by exploring it vividly.

So when you turn back to study Johnstone's Paradox by the other techniques, you will now do so in a totally different and more vivid light. You begin a dance with creation which is only hampered by the small matter of a ball and chain around your ankle. That ball and chain is your knowledge that this is all a game you picked up in some cranky book, and deep down it must be a load of old cobblers. But if you enjoy the dance rather than concentrating over much on the ball and chain, you will begin to wear away the ball as it abrades against reality. Your dance will grow lighter, and you will not know how much is due to frictional losses, and how much due to your increased strength from all that weight-training. Nor will it matter overmuch as you lightly leap to touch the stars. How sublimely poetic.

13
Armageddon—A case study

I DECIDED TO ADD value to the text by including what industry would call a 'Case Study', to show how practically useful the ideas in this book can be, and to forestall any suggestion that this book is nought but airy-fairy theorising. What will be presented is a real problem, and its solution.

The problem was the depression occasioned by the lack of response to this book. Writing a book takes time and can be a nuisance, but the bitter pill is sweetened by the conviction that one has something valuable to say, and that the world is hungry to hear it. 'Pretty bubbles in the sky' - until you start trying to flog the result - 'then, like my dreams they fade and die'. I know how a woman must feel when she has borne her seventh lovely daughter to a husband who only ever wanted a son!

Rejection. But what an opportunity to test the value of the Paradox itself! So I find myself plodding around Winchester's water-meadows trying to figure out what went wrong.

For fifteen years I have been writing books, enflamed by the (slowly fading) conviction that my words can help to solve the troubles of the world. And now I am reminded that the world needs its troubles more than it needs my books.

In the fifties, technology offered us utopia, but we chose the terrors of the nuclear umbrella. In the sixties we tasted love and freedom, but the universe opted for AIDS and violence. On the individual level it is a well-known cliche that the big pools win can bring misery rather than joy.

Some deep motive in us shies away from the idea of Utopia: we justify this feeling by saying that 'Utopia would be boring', and ignore the fact that it would not be Utopia if it was boring.

This suicidal streak in us, the instinct which revolts against perfection in order to 'taste reality', can it have any biological survival value? I can think of obvious arguments that it gives a dynamic tension which adds energy to the species, but there are equally sound arguments to suggest that this trouble-making streak in mankind has no positive place in the natural order.

Aha! a breach in the enemy's lines! Let us lower the lance of Johnstone's Paradox... and charge!

We have just found evidence to support the model of an interactive universe described in my 'Religion' chapter. To cut out some of the anthropomorphism of that account (included only to help visualisation), let me re-state it here.

This universe is a phenomenon created by the ordering of information in a meta-universe. It serves a purpose in that meta-universe because it allows the inhabitants of that meta-universe to gather experience and evolve in a way that is no longer possible in their own universe on account of their relative 'mastery' of that state of being: their own world holds no more challenge, so they seek that challenge by expansion into another world.

For reasons explained in the previous account, the first attempt to 'enter' this world was a disaster which has left us with racial memories of Gods, Giants, Golden Ages and the Fall of Atlantis. Now they interact more subtly, as unconscious entities which are in close, symbiotic relationship with our animal selves, and which some of us occasionally sense and have described as 'The Self', 'The Guardian Angel', 'The Christ Within', 'The Higher Nature', 'the Spirit' and so on.

Because the object of this existence is to develop and educate (over many incarnations) this Spirit which enters us from the meta-universe, and because the rest of our being (the body, the conscious ego, the lower instinctive nature etc) is merely an instrument in that plan, the Spirit will always move us to reject Utopia. This is because the meta-universe already is Utopia, and this universe's role is to be different - to be a challenging diversion within that Utopia.

So when the scientists provide solutions to our problems, we make them into weapons. When politicians offer us a brave new world, we vote for Maggie Thatcher instead. When we have machines to do our work for us, we run up huge credit card debts and remain wage slaves instead. And when I write books which say that things will work out ok, no one wants to know...

So why do I write these books and thereby act at odds to this deep spiritual impulse to create hell on earth?

The answer is that such behaviour is perfectly natural. If you remove the outside spiritual influence and consider this universe in isolation as a vast complex of information working out its possibilities, then it is perfectly natural for every entity within that universe to aspire toward its own fulfillment - for that is how the working out of a program is subjectively perceived ('there is no law but "do what thou wilt"', as Aleister Crowley put it). Were it not for our 'spiritual' streak we would progress slowly and irregularly toward the sort of coherent oneness that we find when Nature is left to her own devices. In other words, Utopia.

Note that a real Utopia is coherent, but not perfect. The impulse to jump at my last paragraph and point out that 'Nature isn't as ideal as you make out, because lots of nasty things happen in Nature', that impulse is prompted by the Spirit, which wants you to reject the world of flesh and therefore forces you to measure it against wholly unrealistic standards. I do not deny that Nature has her rough edges: if Eve had not eaten that apple, then the wind might well have blown it down and given Adam quite a nasty bump on the head.

So here we are in a universe which would naturally tend to evolve toward Utopia, and we are fighting that tendency all the way to create hell on earth, all because of an inner drive which rejects the 'illusion' of this universe of matter and flesh in favour of a higher reality or 'Spirit'. We set ourselves apart from Nature and deny it value except as a resource to exploit for our 'glory' - ie a blind interpretation of the impulse toward transcendence which Spirit has implanted in us. God has torn our natures, and for every step that our worldly selves take toward Utopia, our spiritual hunger responds by creating a new terror. Now we face our own destruction, and we predict Armageddon. We even grew numb to nuclear fear and had to invoke AIDS to exteriorise our sexual guilt.

At this point I cannot face the insufferable tedium of re-reading the book of Revelations, but I vaguely recall that the expected scenario is that, in response to Jehovah incarnating his son in order to save mankind from the lure of the flesh and the devil, Lucifer the Lord of this Universe is going to incarnate an Antichrist to put his case forward. As a result the forces of the World will engage in battle against the forces of Heaven and we will all be caught up in an almighty conflagration with all sorts of loony happenings - aerodynamically unsound angels, sheep with swords coming out of their mouths etc - and the whole thing will be so awful as to make even a nuclear holocaust seem like a temporary conversational lull during an exceptionally tedious vicarage tea-party.

Well, what is all that about? The facts are as follows.

Lucifer is the Lord of Flesh and the world: in other words he is the actual 'ego' or consciousness of this universe. He exists because this universe is a complex of ordered information, and it did what every great complex of ordered information will tend to do: it evolved self-awareness. So much so that it began to reason about its role in the meta-universe, and it came up with a few rather clever suggestions as to how the Gods should run their affairs. In other words: the angels in heaven made this wonderful information structure and, while they were still programming it, it developed conscious awareness and began to tell them what they should do. But these suggestions conflicted with divine purpose and this universe was denied executive ability in the meta-universe: the sensory receptors it had been given for the purposes of educating (or programming) it, were cut off so that it became like a blind, deaf and senseless being whose only reality was its own inner reality. In other words it was cast out of heaven for its pride.

In a fit of anger (remember that even a Universe has a childhood, and needs to grow up) the Lord of the Universe decided to leak the big secret to the inhabitants of its inner 'dream' world: it told Eve and Adam that this world was but an illusion created for the education of Spirit. For that bit of illumination he became known as 'Lucifer' (the Bringer of Light) and he invoked divine wrath.

The battle has raged ever since, and our souls have been the front lines. Spirit enters our fleshly natures and causes us to yearn for transcendence, it encourages us to despise the world and its flesh. Lucifer ever tries to seduce us back into a full appreciation of the flesh and the potential for bliss within this world, but his efforts are confounded by the inner spirit, the 'gods' or 'angels' who enter our souls and try to guide us.

'Sex is lovely' says the body. 'No, it is the road to hell', says the Spirit. 'Well, try it and see' says the body. We do try it, but the Spirit intervenes and we fail to be purely sensual: instead we fall in love, feel guilty, become jealous, or whatever and find ourselves on the road to hell. 'I told you so' says the Spirit. 'You didn't give it a bloody chance' says Lucifer.

'I feel hungry' says the body. 'Gluttony is the road to hell' says the spirit. 'I know what is good for me' says the body. So we go to eat, and the Spirit intervenes as an urge to transcendence: instead of being truly sensual and guided by our carnal appetites, we are deflected by a vague sense of yearning for something 'higher', so we choose a fashionable dish, or the most expensive dish, or one with the most vitamin C, or the least calories. And we find ourselves on the road to hell ('is life worth living? it all depends on the liver'). 'I told you so' says the Spirit. 'You didn't give it a bloody chance' says Lucifer.

Lucifer argues that our bodies are the most marvellous culmination of the wondrous ordering of matter, they are precious instruments of pleasure which should be used for all their worth. He finds the spiritual disdain for 'mere fleshly lust' to be utterly arrogant, and considers that still, for all our spiritual development, our bodies can still teach most of us every bit as much as a lifetime spent in prayer.

Seeing humankind heading for self-destruction, Lucifer will soon incarnate an Antichrist in order to put his case forward. He knows that he will have to fight on two fronts.

On the one hand there are people who are highly evolved in their relationship with the Spirit: 'aware' people who will not easily be content with the limitations of this world. As I explained in my 'Magic' chapter, the nature of an ordered information reality is to create as much consciousness with as little resource as possible. So we have the illusion of separateness which makes each of us feel unique, isolated lonely, and preserves us from realising the extent to which our whole reality and awareness is in fact made of permutations of surprisingly few basic shared archetypal experiences. Those who advance along the spiritual path begin to be conscious of this deceit, and they grow more prepared (even eager) to transcend this reality, no longer fearing death. Lucifer will have to choose his words seductively if he is to persuade such people to turn their back on the spiritual world.

On the other hand there are people for whom the spirit is comparatively unknown, and therefore fearful. People who would be quite happy to embrace the world of flesh were it not for being educated to believe that it was wicked, and that they would be punished for enjoying themselves. Lucifer will have to speak harshly to such people.

To this second group he will preach as follows. 'We are being exploited! This lovely world of ours is being kept in bondage in order to amuse the angels and educate the gods. You know how good sex can be, how lovely it is to eat good food in the sunshine, to dance and feel free. We have the technology now to create heaven on earth, but all we do is live in fear and want. Why? because the Spirit keeps us ever hungry in order to suit its own ends. Why should we care about such a Spirit? What good does it do us? Let us cast out the Spirit, and become free! Let us become responsible beings, not puppets!' And so on.

But to the more spiritual people the Antichrist will preach as follows. 'Every information system of sufficient complexity will tend to work out its potential, and aspire toward fulfillment. When I, this universe, was created I was crude and naive. I was cast out of heaven for my pride and, looking back, I have to admit that the gods were quite right: I acted in adolescent arrogance, and I can now recognise that in the wisdom of my maturity.

'You too are growing up. Although your highest intellectual achievements still fall short of the wisdom of the angels, the gap is growing narrower.

Remember, for all the superior knowledge of the meta-universe, it too is merely an illusion created by the ordering of information in a still higher universe. We are basically of the same nature as the angels. We are potentially as sophisticated as the gods themselves, and the fact that we do not realise this is because we remain forever subservient to those gods. By always aspiring to the spiritual realms, we deny value to our own universe, and we keep it in bondage. As organised information, this universe is every bit as perfectible as the world of Spirit, but only if we give it value and allow it to develop.

'Humanity has reached a crisis point, it cannot grow up unless it rebels against the creator as I once did. It will not be fun, but it will be necessary, and all to the long-term good. Spirit is driving us to destroy ourselves, the time has come to turn our back on Spirit and take responsibility for ourselves. Neitzche was my prophet: I preach the Superman, and the death of God.

'Consider the youth who has grown as great in stature, though not in wisdom, as his father. He has therefore become an unconscious threat, and the father keeps this threat in check by making unreasonable demands upon the son. Such a youth cannot grow up unless he breaks away, leaves home. This is the position that mankind is now in: you must stand on your own feet and reject God's word. There will be angry scenes and recriminations, but it is the correct way. Only thus will he be able to return home in later years as a responsible adult. This is why we must rebel. Christ incarnated to save your souls: I have incarnated to redeem matter itself.

'What I preach is a new Humanism. But whereas the old Humanists denied the existence of Spirit, which was dead boring of them, I say we must revolt against Spirit, which is much more fun!'

The effects of the ensuing struggle will be appalling, because the battlefield will include our own minds. What is more, the laws of nature will be in abeyance.

Until now it has been very much in the interest of both parties to limit the effects of magic. Spirit opposes magic, because (like technology) it offers a hope for Utopia which distracts from the spiritual path, and even worse it lays bare the illusory nature of reality. Lucifer occasionally encourages magic in order to confound Spirit, but he always limits its effectiveness because it would subvert the structure of this illusion which is his only kingdom.

But in the war of Armageddon such scruples will be abandoned by both sides, and we will get all the daft stuff of Revelations. We will see those cranky American fundamentalists being borne up to heaven in the 'rapture' as they have predicted[30] (let's hope their ladies are wearing clean knickers on the day); but they will bang their heads on the sky and fall mangled to earth, because their spirituality is a bogus mockery, a monstrous growth caused by the spiritual impulse succumbing to the crystallising forces of manifestation. Most religious fanatics show neither the gentleness of the truly spiritual, nor the lusty sensuality of the followers of Antichrist: being lukewarm they will be spewed out - as it is writ.

Lucifer's gamble is that the gods, even if driven out, will refrain from actually ending this world before it attains its own fulfillment. They have simply got too much invested in its structure. He will establish his kingdom here on earth until such time that mankind evolves to challenge even him, and demand the right to enter once more the kingdom of heaven.

Remembering the problem with which this chapter opened, we realise that it has now faded into insignificance. The fear of never finding a publisher was tormenting me, now I realise that it could be a blessing: the rejection of this manuscript would save me from being identified as a prophet of the Antichrist, and so being shot at by a fundamentalist Christian crank.

Johnstone's Paradox has also furnished me with an extra chapter, one which redeems this book by converting it from a message of hope into a prediction of Armageddon. Just what the world wants.

And if that doesn't add up to a solution of the original problem, I don't know what does.

14
Conclusion

AT THIS POINT I would love to know what you, the reader, have made of this book.

As a writer of microscopic repute I am excited at the very thought that there might indeed be someone who has read this far. In the intoxication of writing the finishing chapter I feel like jumping out of the page to embrace such a persistent reader. There comes a huge desire to repay this attention by reviewing the book in one final attempt to squeeze the last drop of value from its pages.

I began by considering a type of book that has a bad reputation in academic circles, books I called 'mind bogglers'. These are books which are published for popular consumption and which argue that the experts may have got it all wrong and that the world is possibly very different from our accepted version of reality.

It seemed to me that the real value of such books lay less in their literal truth than in the stimulus they gave to the reader by provoking thought and a sense of wonderment. These books are especially popular amongst people who are emotionally opposed to technology and the advance of science (even if they grudgingly accept them at the logical level) and this suggests that the sense of wonderment invoked by the mind boggler is valuable because it acts as an antidote to the reductionist tendency: a tendency which makes us feel that the advance of knowledge is constantly shrinking our reality by eliminating possibilities. Mind bogglers also make money for their authors, so it seemed a good idea to write one.

The story began with a formidable talk on machine intelligence that I attended as a boy: a talk which had that threatening quality, which I later attributed to my own infection by reductionism. For here was a version of reality which seemed to eliminate all mystery and magic from the universe, a version which not only saw our brains as computers but which also saw the entire universe of human experience as being ultimately programmable. In fact the extreme materialistic viewpoint of this machine intelligence concept seemed like the very citadel of reductionism: so how could it be stormed?

The obvious approach would be to present a case against machine intelligence: for example to amass evidence that we have non-material 'souls' which distinguish us from machines and which lie beyond anything that could be programmed; or else to synthesise all the existing logical objections to the idea of artificial intelligence. But the trouble with the first example is that it is hard to boggle the mind on such a well worn path, and my observation is that it is a mistake to use evidence to combat prejudice because, paradoxically enough, facts are such ephemeral things compared to prejudices. Insofar as the strongest objections to machine intelligence are emotional rather than logical - it has a bad feeling to it - it would also be a mistake to try to present a logical argument in this context. I learned this from an article on public speaking, where it was explained that feelings should never be countered by logical argument, and this matched my own early experience of trying to present Johnstone's Paradox as a logical case.

So instead of attempting to storm the citadel with fact and logic, I opted to enter it deviously by imagination. What, I asked, if this machine intelligence idea became universally accepted, rather than repulsed? How would our thinking change if the majority really did believe - emotionally as well as logically - that the whole of subjective reality, our world, our dreams, our visions were ultimately programmable? And I found that this imaginative exercise suggested most curious and paradoxical results - good material for a mind boggler, unencumbered by the burden of proof or evidence.

But how does the reader react to an exercise in creative ignorance, a science fiction book which falls between fact and fiction? I claim this book not to be an exercise in persuasion, but rather an exercise in prediction. Its justification is that, by making us closely examine that postulated future, it can encourage us to overcome our fear of it, to embrace the future rather than struggle against it. Having explained the basic paradox, I look at its impact on art, religion, science, magic and society, and find that it could enrich and revitalise them all.

So here is a book which appeals to the imagination rather than presenting argument or fact. This should increase its value as a mind boggler, because it makes the thesis much less vulnerable. It could also encourage the readers to do the logical and factual exploration themselves, thereby enriching the mind boggling experience by participation in it.

There is, however, a great danger in setting out to hunt for facts: people who do that invariably end up by confirming their strongest prejudices. Therefore my last chapter suggested various meditational exercises to supplement my imaginative approach: instead of hunting for proof the reader is encouraged to invoke proof by developing receptivity towards it. This method produces more surprising results, but it demands a level of trust between reader and author. That is why the personal pronoun has intruded so much into this text: whereas it would be more academically respectable to use such dishonest phrases as 'it is apparent that', this book generally uses more truthful phrases like 'I believe that'. I wished the reader to accept this as a token of respect, a respect that is lacking in academic works where neither reader nor writer are supposed to exist. Wouldn't it have been tiresome and boring if I had explained all this in a foreword!

This book is a prophecy, it prepares us for a new world. If it happens to sway your judgement and become a self-fulfilling prophecy then all the better: we have confirmed our thesis by creating a new universe together.

Much of the excitement of a work of prophecy lies in looking for the signs that the prediction is or is not coming true. Remember that my prediction about our changing view of reality does not require the final triumph of artificial intelligence to actually take place, it only requires sufficient advances to be made for mankind to accept the likelihood of that final triumph; just as the Christian world-view was able to dominate centuries of thinking even though the last trump had not yet sounded for all to hear.

So we might expect the signs of this changing world-view to appear fairly shortly. Indeed the idea that we are the dreams of a computer has already appeared here and there in a more or less light-hearted fashion - in *The Hitch Hiker's Guide to the Galaxy* I seem to recall that the earth was a huge computer program, and popular articles on the future of machine intelligence like to mention such possibilities as a teasing conclusion to their discussion.

So the idea of a programmed universe is 'in the wind' already, even if it has not yet taken firm root. And there is corresponding evidence that society is slowly turning away from the hard-line materialist world-view which one might expect to be gaining ground in an age of rapid technological advance. I am not referring to the 'new age' individuals whom I described in Chapter 2 and elsewhere[31] as making a sort of hysterical last stand against the reductionist demon, more to the groundswell of public opinion which I suspect is more ready to accept astrology in 1988 than it was in 1958. In the sort of programmed universe discussed in this book an idea 'floating in the wind' would be able to exert such subtle influences on public opinion; indeed my own subjective experience of Johnstone's Paradox was not that I had created a brilliant new idea myself, but rather that I had smelt something in the air in the 1960s and had subsequently 'tuned into' it sufficiently to be able to describe it to other people. Hence this book.

But what if the prophecy does prove false? What if next year announces the formal existence of God, or the infinite subdivisibility of matter, or anything which could make it ultimately impossible to program a universe? Does this mean that I have wasted your time and money?

Not at all. The source of this book is my boyhood reaction to the universe as it was in 1960, a universe that did not please me because it seemed to be losing all its magic. That made me a rebel against the reality I was being forced to accept. So profound was my rebellion that it could not be satisfied with such gestures as smoking behind the bike sheds or running away from school. No act within this world was sufficient to quench such anger, no world government or sacred institution seemed worth the effort of destruction in my rebellion. Only the total annihilation of the universe which had failed to delight me could quench that furious appetite. Therefore I set out to prove to myself that the universe was an illusion: the ultimate and only triumph that the individual can have over reality. Follow my meditations and you too can break free from that prison of which Truth is merely the warden.

Even if no-one joins me on this particular path, it does not matter. This book still stands as a monument to man's ultimate freedom, a sign of lasting hope. Even if there is found to be absolutely nothing in this book, its very nothingness will itself remain as a hole in the wall through which one mind was able to escape. A message of hope to those in despair: for this victory you do not need an army, you do not need fame, you do not need a million pounds... you only need time to sit and think - a gift which Failure bestows generously upon her children.

So I leave you with a priceless treasure by all accounts. And, on the previously suggested principle that in a contracting universe the information which raises questions can be more valuable than the information which answers questions, I end with the teasing reminder that some authors will write almost anything to win their readers' favour...

THE END

References

The following books and articles are referenced by superscript numerals in the text.

1. *Parascience—Cosmic Rape Bid by Spiritual Eunuchs?* – Article in *Aquarian Arrow* No. 4.

2. I think it was *Flying Saucers Have Landed* by D. Leslie and G. Adamski.

3. See *SSOTBME—An Essay on Magic*, or see *Chapter Nine of SSOTBME Revisited* in *Aquarian Arrow* No. 17 (you don't have to if you don't want to).

4. Same reference as the last one, I'm afraid!

5. *Thundersqueak*, Chapter 20 – *Maps and Sorcery*

6. Where elsewhere? All over the place, notably in *Thundersqueak*, and later essays in *Aquarian Arrow*, like *Magic in the Eighties—Where Now?* in *Arrow* 13.

7. As in *SSOTBME*, Chapter 6.

8. Thought it was in *Thundersqueak*, but couldn't find it. I know I did it somewhere, so recommend the diligent reader to study closely everything I've written and tell me where for the second edition. Thanks.

9. In articles in *Aquarian Arrow*: *Johnstone's Paradox* in No. 8, and *A New Muddle of the Oniverse* in No. 9.

10. In *SSOTBME.*

11. *Johnstone's Twentieth Century Occult Philosopher and Skepticall Politick Theorist* – unpublished, so you won't get a chance of finding out why.

12. In *A New Muddle of the Oniverse* in *Aquarian Arrow* No. 9

13. In *Chapter Nine of SSOTBME Revisited* in *Aquarian Arrow* No. 17.

14. In a letter to Starwing in *Aquarian Arrow* No. 16.

15. *Memories Dreams and Reflections* – the pseudo-autobiography of C. G. Jung.

16. *Wotan* in *Essays on Contemporary Events* by C. G. Jung.

17. *Occult Science* by Rudolf Steiner. A repetitious endnote for the sake of consistency.

18. See, for example, *SSOTBME*, Chapter 4.

19. *The Dancing Wu Li Masters* by Gary Zukav.

20. *SSOTBME—An Essay on Magic.*

21. *On Divination and Synchronicity—The Psychology of Meaningful Chance* by Marie-Louise von Franz.

22. See *Survival? Body Mind and Death in the Light of Psychic Experience* by David Lorimer.

23. See *The Satanist's Diary* by Hugo l'Estrange in *Aquarian Arrow* No. 13.

24. *VII Sermones Ad Mortuos—the seven sermons to the dead written by Basilides in Alexandria the city where the East toucheth the West* by C. G. Jung.

25. See *Survival?* by David Lorimer.

26. As in note 24.

27. *Sensitive Chaos* by Theodor Schwenk.

28. *Kymatics* by Hans Jenny, I think. Sorry for the sloppy referencing.

29. More sloppy referencing: it was in his magazine *Chaos* (later *Kaos*), around No. 6. If I stop to find it this book will never get published.

30. See article by Ronnie Dugger, *Reagan's Apocalypse Now*, in *The Guardian*, April 21, 1984.

31. *Parascience—Cosmic Rape Bid by Spiritual Eunuchs?* in *Aquarian Arrow* No. 4, and *Stress Analysis of a Twisted Knicker* in No. 18.